AdveNtuRe PLay

Adventure Activities for Preschool and Early Elementary Age Children

Nancy MacPhee Bower

Project Adventure, Inc.

Published in conjunction with
Simon & Schuster Custom Publishing

SIMON & SCHUSTER CUSTOM PUBLISHING

Printed in the United States of America

10 9 8 7 6 5 4 3 2 1

Please visit our website at www.sscp.com

ISBN 0–536–01420-5
BA 98510

SIMON & SCHUSTER CUSTOM PUBLISHING
160 Gould Street/Needham Heights, MA 02494
Simon & Schuster Education Group

Dedication

This book is dedicated to the memory of
my niece Jaimie Lee Gates . . . playful
child, joyful dancer.

Contents

Foreword

The world needs more moms, dads and teachers that know how to play. Play is a social phenomena and without some guidance, enthusiasm and playful participation from a child's care givers—parents, teachers, after school providers—Game Boys, Mortal Kombat and the tube may find another friend. Eye-hand coordination and canned video buddies are emphasized at the expense of real learnings that happen when children play together—compassion (mutual respect), caring, decision making, communication, cooperation and the simple enjoyment of goofing around with other like-minded people who want to goof around too. "Yeah, but video games are fun." Help!

Help's here. Nancy Bower (A mom, Project Adventure National Trainer, and friend) knows how to play and does a fine job in this book of passing along those things you need to know to become a playmate. This is a book about how to play with children, not how to entertain them. Nancy offers easily understandable rationale for adventurous fun and gives clear and numerous examples and insights into how adventure activities work with young children.

Nancy's writing style puts a knowledgeable friend at your elbow. Her insights and suggestions are based on experience with children, not pedantic research. Her child-play examples are pertinent and poignant, further emphasizing the real-life aspect of the text.

I could write more supportive things, because the following pages are rich with ideas and usable notions, but I'm just keeping you from the fun. Try a couple of games today and see how well this stuff works. Be childlike (not childish) and enjoy one of the great free experiences of this life time—playing with children.

Karl Rohnke, 1998

Preface

Several years ago, I sat in our family room with my daughter Maggie, three years, and son Freddy, one and a half years old at the time. Though we were surrounded by toys of all kinds, I must admit I was bored. I am almost certain my children were, too. The day felt long already, and it was only 10:30 in the morning.

What is wrong with me? I wondered. I have two wonderful children, we should be having more fun than this. The answer came to me quickly... I had no idea how to play with my children! As an adventurer by profession, I had successfully played games with adults, pre-teens and teenagers for days on end. My situation that day, confronted with my so-called professional expertise caused me much confusion, frustration and even embarrassment. I needed to do something—soon. There were hours and hours left in my day; there were years of hang out time with toddlers and preschoolers ahead of me!

In desperation, I went out to my garage, dug out my game bag—a bag full of toys and props I use in workshops and other adventure events. This had collected considerable dust over the previous months of time off for early motherhood.

I brought the bag into the family room, opened it up and let Maggie and Freddy explore its contents. They pulled out polyspots, fleece balls, ropes, rubber chickens, scarves, dice ... and myriad other items that had not been a part of our toy collection. A vibrancy and giddy energy emerged and our day was transformed—yawns turned into laughter, our dragging feet began leaping and hopping, heavy sighs were now yelps and screeches. The fun factor shot through the roof.

Maggie took a short rope and squiggled it, Freddy jumped over the wiggling rope. "It's a worm!" Maggie shouted. I took over the task of wiggling the worm, the game that brought us into a new way of playing together. From that moment on, I watched the way Maggie and Freddy, and eventually our next daughter, Katherine and many other children played. I took note of what motivated and captivated them. I joined them in their imaginative additions to games. Children have taught me a great deal about play. They have also taught me how to be *playfull*.

Not long after that transformation, Tom Zierk, head of Project Adventure's Publications Department, put out a request for book ideas. I immediately responded with a phone call to Tom. We discussed the fact that very young children—preschoolers and early elementary ages—were somewhat neglected in our Project Adventure publications and workshops. There certainly seemed to be a need for written information on adventure games for very young children. Tom was enthusiastic from the beginning, having implemented many games sessions with his sons' preschool and kindergarten classes. Lisa Furlong, editor and author, enthusiastically joined forces with us to make this book come to life. She had been playing games with elementary students as well as her son's preschool program and also recognized the need for more resources in this area of adventure play for young children.

Tom, Lisa and I began to pool our experiences of games playing with young children. I moved into high gear and began playing games with preschools and after school programs, expanding what we knew, adapting, creating and gathering games from other sources.

Playing with children is a gift we can give to our children and to ourselves—any time, anywhere. The feelings, the fun, the connection and the laughter stay with them for days and even years. All of us have play memories that are decades old, yet are as vivid as if they were played yesterday. The opportunity to create more of these memories is as close as our living rooms and our back doors.

A fellow Project Adventure trainer spotted this poem on a plaque at a children's museum somewhere in her travels. It has remained with me ever since I read it. . . .

I tried to teach my child with words
They passed her over unheard
I tried to teach my child with books
He gave me only puzzled looks
Despairingly I turned aside
"How shall I teach this child?" I cried
Into my hands she put the key
"Come," she said, "Play with me."

author unknown

Enjoy the games that follow. It is my hope that they will transform your backyard, playground and classroom time with your children and students as much as they have mine. Let them be only the beginning of more ideas and games of your own. And don't forget to pass them on. . . .

Peace,

NMB

Acknowledgments

The experience of writing this book has put me onto the very beginning of an enormous learning curve. There are many resources "out there," in the classrooms, homes, neighborhoods and playgrounds. They are the teachers, parents, providers and especially the children we see daily. It has been my goal these past several years to be a gatherer, a sponge and occasionally even an innovator of play ideas.

Many people have helped me along this continuum of growth in the area of adventure play. Most especially I have my children to thank for their inspiration to play... Maggie and Freddy were there for the initial revelation that there are more ways to play than what the toy department stores can provide. Indeed, together we have discovered that the best ways to play cannot be store bought. Our daughter Katherine was born in the midst of the writing of this book. She has joined her brother and sister in the ranks of resident adventure play experts. I have no doubt that my understanding of how to play will grow as they grow into and through the various stages of childhood.

Bob, my friend, husband, and fellow adventurer in life has been a true partner in this book. From the beginning, he has been supportive of this idea, always encouraging me to move forward and make my ideas real. His faith in me and in this project have been a constant source of strength. Some of our family's most connected, most happy and most loving times are those in which we are playing together. Whether we are wrestling, dancing or playing *Sticky Buddies* and *Sleepy Snakes* we are creating wonderful moments that strengthen our family. I am blessed to have a husband and friend who brings playfulness and adventure into our lives.

I would like to thank Tom Zierk, my editor, for being such an advocate for this book.

Tom's enthusiasm and initial "thumbs up" on the idea made it possible to move forward. My writing skills are both rusty and rudimentary. Tom's encouragement and belief that I could actually do the writing helped me embark on this book adventure.

Lisa Furlong, also an editor of this book, worked closely with me for a great deal of the writing phase. She is passionate about this topic and her excitement about the book always energized me when the process seemed to be dragging and the notion of this ever becoming a real book felt more like a fantasy than a reality. The editorial expertise of both Lisa and Tom are woven into the book. I am grateful for all of their guidance and input.

Several preschools and after school programs allowed me to come into their classrooms to test out games and activities. The development phase of this book was certainly the most educational, but also, for me the most fun. Children are constantly learning, playing and growing. This vibrant energy pours out of them and is literally contagious to me. I always came away from a play session energized and rejuvenated. Their teachers are equally energizing and creative and I learned so much from them.

I especially would like to thank the staff and students at the Winfield Children's Center in Falmouth, Maine. I spent many hours with them in the development phase of writing this book. Kathy Black and Liz Standon and their staff made me feel truly "at home," one of the family. Their peaceful, respectful approach with children is a living model of what Project Adventure calls the Full Value Contract.

I would also like to thank the teachers and students at the following schools that allowed me to visit and play games on a regular basis:

The Preble Resource Center, Portland, Maine, especially Amy Sidel, Althea Hall and Karen Silverman

The P.R.O.P. Head Start Program, Cumberland, Maine, especially Kelly Burgess and Carolyn Ramsey

The P.R.O.P. Head Start Program, Sagamore Village, Portland, Maine

The Cumberland Community Cooperative Nursery School, Cumberland, Maine, especially Ellen Gagnon

The Pine Grove Children's Center, Falmouth, Maine, especially B.J. Fifield and Kate Molloy

The Portland Recreation Department After school Program, Reiche School, Portland, Maine, especially Dave Caldwell

Michelle Stuckey, Casco Bay Movers in Portland, Maine

Tom Zierk and Lisa Furlong played and tested games with preschools and kindergarten classes to assist in the development of this book.

We are grateful for the contributions of the staff and students at: Driscoll School in Brookline, MA and the staff at the Cuvilly Earth and Arts Center, in Ipswich, MA.

I would also like to thank my friends who came out on a very cold March day to play games and to be photographed:

Griffin and David Googins-Gorski, Rebecca and Anna Curtis-Heald, Robbie and Chan Arndt, Gregory and Megan Smith, Maggie Bower and Rosita and Christine Reighley.

I would also like to thank those who contributed their photographic skills:

David Heald, Cumberland, Maine

Tom Zierk, Publications Director, Project Adventure

Rufus Collinson, Editor, Project Adventure

Janet Goodman for designing the book and adding the illustrations.

Karl Rohnke has inspired me for years with his playful spirit. He creates fun wherever he goes and I have been fortunate to have "worked" in his company quite often. My library is filled with his books to which I migrate when I need ideas and a jump start to my games repertoire. Not only do I find inspiration in his words, but reliably, I will also get a good chuckle. I found myself consulting with Karl quite often in the process of writing this book. In our many check-in conversations he gave me clear, honest feedback and advice, lots of encouragement and always a good dose of fun!

Marianne Torbert, Ph.D., author and professor at Temple University, is definitely the most exciting discovery I have made throughout this project. She has written several books on movement activities for young children: Including *Follow Me, Too* (Addison Wesley Publishers) and *Follow Me, A Handbook of Movement Activities For Children* (Leonard Gordon Institute at Temple University, Philadelphia, PA). I highly recommend that you include these in your library of resources if you don't own them already. We have had many conversations and we finally met when I took a course taught by her. She has educated and inspired me as well as many others who work in this field. I am honored to have had her read the draft of this book and provide me with feedback.

Finally, I would like to thank Carrie Sawyer who cared for and nurtured my children whenever I needed to work on this book. She has become a special part of our lives. Her crafts bag of tricks has provided Maggie, Freddy and Katherine with many adventures in art that they love and cherish.

Introduction

This book is for anyone who works with young children—parents, teachers, child care providers, troop leaders, camp counselors, after school teachers. It is a book of games, a resource that I hope will stimulate ideas that will move you and your children toward more adventurous, more creative and more cooperative play.

Toddlers, preschoolers, early elementary ages—these children are the purest of players, the play experts. They know how to play as well as they know how to breathe. They play for a living. They learn by playing. They often solve their problems through play. They are masters in the art of playing for fun, for the sheer joy of it. For young children, the very act of playing is the most important reason for playing... not the outcome, not the score or the measuring of the fastest time, not the winning or being the best. They become completely absorbed in play.

What to Expect in this Book

Adventure Play is divided into two sections. Section One offers some guidelines and background to the philosophy and practice of adventure education—a field whose value is increasingly recognized by teachers, therapists, physical educators, camp counselors, corporate trainers, clergy and Sunday school teachers, social workers, and a myriad of professionals who work with groups of people.

While some readers will want to jump right to the activities, which begin in Section Two, the knowledge gained by reading and understanding the information in Section One, especially Chapter One, will make a big difference in how you present the activities and ultimately the learning gained by the children in your group. To paraphrase Karl Rohnke, the games master who has written the best selling adventure games and activities books, without an understanding of what it is you are presenting and how to process the learnings from the activities, you are offering merely entertaining recreation. Which may be a goal in itself, but adventure activities also offer groups a chance to learn, in fun, nonthreatening ways how to cooperate better, how to value all members of the group, how to solve problems together, and how to better understand and get along with others—all valuable lessons that are learned through the adventure play experience. The success of the games presented in Section Two can be significantly impacted by our actions and messages. The information provided in Section One provides the tools you can use to guide your adventures in a positive direction.

Section One—Adventure Play

The three chapters in this section help you understand the why and how of adventure education. Chapter One presents The Basics and introduces the very cornerstones of adventure education. Challenge by Choice is a philosophy that encourages you to offer children choices. It is a philosophy that reminds all of us that what is not challenging for one person may be very challenging for another. The Full Value Contract is a teaching strategy that supports the process of learning to work with others. With a Full Value Contract young children learn what it means to play with kindness, consideration and respect for others.

Chapter Two presents a series of commonly asked questions and my best response to them. After leading many, many hour of adventure activities and games with young children, I have come to anticipate a number of common pitfalls and areas of concern. Chapter Three walks you through some sample program ideas to help you incorporate the games and activities into your own setting.

Section Two—The Activities

There are four categories of games and activities in this book. Within each category are activities that require varying levels of physical skill and activity. Each activity has a key which lets you know how much space you'll need and what props are necessary.

Body Skills, Stretches and Warm-Ups

These are activities that help young children develop specific physical skills. Through games that require moving and playing together, your children will also learn to play safely and with kindness.

Buddy Games

Games to play with two's, three's and more are valuable for learning early cooperation and communication skills.

Running, Jumping, Fast Moving Games

Children love and need to run. They often appear their happiest and most vibrant when allowed to stretch and work legs and lungs and hearts.

Problem Solving and Trust Building Activities

These activities help children continue to develop their cooperative skills. By emphasizing problem solving and trust development, you'll find your group playing in a whole new way.

Circle Games

Just making a circle can often be a challenge, but these fun, cooperative games give your children the chance to begin playing as a larger group.

Section One

Adventure Play

Chapter One

An Introduction To Adventure

Watch children on a playground. You see running, jumping, skipping, singing and a whole lot of creativity. Slides become slippery mountains and swings become airplanes. But within these moments of play, children are also learning. *Adventure Play* is about using this natural desire for play and physical movement to teach. It is

about helping children to see that the way they play is important, to see that working together cooperatively, safely and kindly is ultimately more fun.

Adventure Play...

- focuses on cooperation more than competition
- challenges the individual to try new behaviors and new skills
- encourages small groups of children to work together
- promotes exploration and enjoyment of the environment
- involves all players and *does not eliminate anyone*
- offers opportunities for everyone at their own skill level
- does not highlight certain players as better or less skilled than others

Most importantly, adventure play is creative and fun.

Adventure play transforms the playground, neighborhood, classroom or living room into a place where fun, challenge, learning and new opportunities and insights are possible.

Learning to Play and Playing to Learn

Children need to play independently. They also need to learn to deal with more structured settings. As parents and teachers we strive for a balance of structured and unstructured learning opportunities. The games in this book initially require a facilitator. Each experience presents an adventure of its own. The potential learnings and challenges contained within each activity are numerous. If we plant the seed, the children feed it with their own imaginations—and surely, it will grow into something unexpected and quite wonderful.

Cooperation is not a skill that develops overnight. It is not like the ability to hop or skip that, once developed, stays with us forever. Even adults are often challenged by the decision to cooperate or not to cooperate. We learn to cooperate when we experience the benefits and satisfaction that working together brings. As educators and parents, we can facilitate our children's movement along a continuum of growth in learning how to cooperate with others.

Adventure play not only helps children learn to work together, it provides opportunities to run and jump and move around. It offers the chance for growth—to learn a new physical skill, to help others, to practice sharing and communicating. Using Adventure, you will engage your young group in a fun learning experience.

How wonderful that so much growth and learning can take place through fun and games!

Competition vs Cooperation

Some people thrive on competition, others want nothing to do with it. In fact, for some people, competitive play diminishes the spirit and sense of self. We all fall somewhere along this broad spectrum.

Competition can be exciting, rewarding and physically beneficial. I personally love participating in team sports—the camaraderie, the sweating, the striving for the win. A unique and wonderful part of me comes alive in competitive play settings. But put me on a field with players whose skill level far exceeds my own and that unique and wonderful part is nowhere to be found.

There are many opportunities today for younger and younger children to participate in organized team sports—preschool soccer and toddler t-ball can be found in many communities. To win and to try to be better than others are values children begin learning at an early age. Unfortunately, many young children learn that they are not as skilled as others in sports and games. Adventure activities provide a unique and valuable alternative for competitive games and sports. Adventure activities utilize all players, value the contributions of each member of the group and give children opportunities to increase their skills and challenge themselves in ways in which they are ready.

Adventure Learning Goals

The developmental differences even among children of the same age are tremendous. One child may be very skilled verbally, another physically and yet another socially. Meeting the needs of all of these children within one curriculum is challenging. Many schools address the issue by offering choices—work stations, free play, reading corners, etc. What is wonderful about adventure games is that the varied skills and needs of the children enhance the quality of the experience.

Adventure activities tend to provide several levels of challenge within any one activity. If we pay attention to the children's varied needs for challenge, we can offer games in which no child is bored from being under-challenged, and no children are so over-challenged that they feel intimidated.

There is much to learn in the games you will find in this book. What your children learn will depend upon the skills necessary to have a successful experience with a particular activity. For example, in the game *Hoop Tunnel*, children form a tunnel using hula hoops. Individually and with partners, they pass through the tunnel. The challenge for one child may be in holding up the hoops. For another child the challenge may be to crawl on all fours. Another child will need to speed up her pace in order to feel challenged. Others will be challenged to be more aware of their partners. The learning opportunities in this one simple activity are endless. It will be up to you to observe each child carefully, intervening and questioning as needed. As a facilitator, you will have many opportunities to restructure the activity to meet the needs of the children. I have discovered that children revise games automatically according to their own needs.

Some of the basic skills covered in all the games include—

- working with other children; social skills for connecting with others
- communicating, being able to express emotions and share ideas
- movement skills, both gross and fine motor
- early learning about cooperation and problem solving, sequencing tasks and helping each other toward a common goal
- trusting in oneself and others
- solving conflicts

The Basics

As educators, our first task is to create an environment that promotes learning. In order to learn, no matter what the skill or subject, certain essential conditions must exist. These are:

- Trust
- Safety
- Support
- Respect
- Choices

When these conditions exist, children thrive and learning becomes an enjoyable process in which they are eager to be involved.

Our first task, as teachers, is to lay the groundwork that puts these conditions into action. Most likely, you already have some ground rules or guidelines for your classroom. Project Adventure has several tools that are effective in helping individuals and groups establish a sense of trust, safety, support, respect and choices.

These tools are:

The Full Value Contract

One of the fundamental concepts that Project Adventure uses in all group work is the Full Value Contract. The essence of the Full Value Contract is that all people have the right to be valued—their opinions, thoughts and feelings. This valuing includes both physical safety and emotional well-being, as well as the notion that valuing oneself is as important as valuing others. For some people, valuing themselves can be a great deal more difficult than valuing others.

When used with older children and adults, the FVC is usually developed by the group. Together, they brainstorm ways in which they can become a healthy, happy and caring community. It may take the form of a piece of paper that everyone signs or a poster on the wall listing ways in which a group agrees to work together.

Some programs and schools have adopted this concept so completely that they consider themselves Full Value Schools or Full Value Workplaces. We certainly can extend the concept into any environment—The Full Value Playground, Full Value Scout Troop, Full Value After School Program, Full Value Child Care Center...

Play Hard, Play Safe, Play Fair is one version of the Full Value Contract that has become widely used in many programs. These three phases encompass the essential ingredients of a Full Value Contract—participating to your fullest ability, taking care of others and taking care of yourself.

These three ideas, however, are often too abstract for preschoolers and early elementary grade children, who operate on very concrete terms. *Hard* is a rock, *safe* is in your mom's or dad's arms and *fair* is where you go to ride the Ferris wheel.

In order for young children to understand the Full Value Contract, I present it as three simple statements:

•Be Gentle

•Be Kind

•Be Safe

Be Gentle

Be Gentle focuses on the *physical* aspects of play. Games can be very active without being aggressive and involving rough contact. In many ways, Being Gentle is sort of an ongoing effort in spotting. Spotting, in other adventure activities, is the role participants play to ensure everyone's safety—whether a person is balancing on a log, being lifted up by others or involved in a fast-moving tag game. The spotters have their hands ready to break a possible fall or avoid a rough bump with another participant. The ultimate job of the spotters is to guarantee that others do not get hurt. Being Gentle, in this respect, is about each person being responsible for keeping others safe from physical harm.

No matter how well you think your group has understood and agreed to work at their Full Value Contract, many opportunities will arise to deepen their understanding of the concepts, especially to Be Gentle. To reinforce their understanding, you can call FREEZE to stop the action and then quietly remind the children of their agreement and the need to be gentle with others. Or you can simply pose a question: "I wonder how well we are doing at Being Gentle?" I often gently touch a child on the head or the arm as I remind them so that they have a physical connection to understanding gentleness.

Be Kind

Be Kind is about taking care of one another's feelings and emotions and requires some communication skills to bring it to life. Much of what children communicate

to each other in playground play, especially as they get older, is often negative. I will ask a child if they think the words they are using are kind. Even very young children are almost always aware of the negative impact their words have on others. "Sara deserves kind words," is a reminder of the Full Value Contract. "How did it feel to hear those words, Sara?"

Role modeling supportive language goes a long way in demonstrating ways to Be Kind. When you see a child helping out another, acknowledge that kindness. If you continue to tell your children that they are doing a good job and use an emphatic YES! they will readily adopt similar messages and use them with each other without prompting.

Be Safe

Be Safe is about following the *rules of the game*. The rules are very specific to each activity you play and to the area in which you are playing. For example, in some games there is no running, or only two people are chasing each other at a time. Be sure to state these safety guidelines simply and clearly before you begin a game. You may need to call a time out to restate any safety rules or even revise the game if children are not following them.

Safety guidelines also need to be appropriate to the group's developmental abilities. For example, boundary markers may be wider for an older group needing lots of room to run. A younger group may need more obvious boundaries, such as a rope shaped into a square as opposed to cones marking four corners with imaginary lines drawn in between.

Present these three concepts to your group according to their developmental level. At the start of every game session, revisit your group's Full Value Contract. With all age groups, it is helpful to review each of the guidelines—Be Gentle, Be Kind, Be Safe—and ask, "What does Be Gentle look like? What does Be Kind sound like? What can you do to Be Safe in this group?" Children often find it easier to tell you what each notion is not. Being Gentle is not pushing, Being Kind is not calling names, Being Safe is not running into people.

Before playing a game you can emphasize one of the concepts. "This game is really going to make us work at our gentleness because we have to tag each other very softly." Even after you have been using the activities for a while with your group, the three pieces of the Full Value Contract need consistent reinforcement and reviewing.

Challenge By Choice ... or Growing My Way

Challenge By Choice is the second fundamental Project Adventure operating principle. Developed in the 1970's it has since become the foundation upon which many adventure based programs are built. The basic idea is that individuals choose when and how they will challenge themselves, or, as I like to think of it, when and how they grow. To adults, what may appear to be an easy (unchallenging) activity, can be a huge challenge for a child. For example, the activity *The Clock* appears to be a nonthreatening, simple game, but some children prefer to stand back and observe it being played. The reaction of many adults to such a choice might be that "Tricia's not playing, she is missing out. This is a loss for her (or a disappointment for me)."

But if I am teaching with a Challenge By Choice philosophy, my reaction has a totally different framing. Tricia is saying, through her actions, *I am growing my way.* Through the Challenge by Choice lens, I perceive her behavior and tell myself, "Tricia is observing and that is her way of actively participating." She may be gathering information she needs in order to feel ready and safe enough to play. I respect Tricia for choosing how she wants to grow. Our role as teachers is to play a supportive part in helping children move in incremental steps toward individual goals.

Tricia needs to hear from her teacher that her decision to observe is respected and that help is available to her whenever she is ready to join the circle. Preschoolers and kindergartners need and enjoy repetition, so the more you play a game, the safer children will feel.

The playground slide may seem daunting for many preschoolers. While sitting at the top of the slide and looking down may be one child's success, just standing on the bottom rung of the ladder may be another's. Even well-intentioned coaxing can feel threatening to a child. The fear and anxiety a child feels at those moments of challenge cannot be overridden by comments such as:

- Of course you can do that. What are you crying for?
- Katie can do this and she's even younger than you.
- Just do it and stop being a baby.
- This is easy. You shouldn't be afraid of this.
- You're missing out on a lot of fun.

Rather, we can say…

- What is it like for you at the top of the slide? What are you feeling?
- How can I help you? Would you like me to hold your hand as you slide?

- Would you like me to slide down with you?
- You did a great job climbing to the top!

Many adults have memories of experiences when they were forced or coerced into doing something. Think back to your own childhood and recall the feelings related to those forced experiences. Whether the outcome was positive or negative, the process no doubt also came with some pain, sadness, humiliation or even anger. On the other hand, those endeavors that you chose and pursued on your own brought rewards without the arm-twisted, backed-into-a-corner feeling. The rewards most likely were pride, a positive sense of self and a feeling of true success… "I did it!" versus "You made me do it."

Invite children to try new experiences. Encourage them to join in if they seem withdrawn or hesitant. A *participate or else* approach will only push a child further away. Revise the game if it makes children more comfortable. A game or activity that appears quite basic can be divided into several pieces to meet the developmental needs of all the children. Praise them for attempting a new activity. Identify that it must have been difficult, scary, uncomfortable, whatever the case may be, for them to do what they did.

Sharing

Challenge By Choice is a very helpful philosophy when it comes to the very challenging concept of sharing. Sharing is a developmental skill that comes slowly to children and certainly comes and goes unpredictably. It is a challenge for many older children, and it is nearly impossible for most two- and three-year-olds. If a child does not feel that their toy is safe, if they do not trust that the other child will take care of their toy, they will not be ready to share. Framed this way, it is easy to understand that forcing a child to share is about as effective as pushing a nervous child down the slide.

Certainly the same conditions of safety and trust necessary for a child to freely choose to go down the slide also exist for a child to share their possessions. Imagine the child's relief when his teacher respects his decision by saying, "Greg, you're not ready to share the ball, are you?" As a teacher, you can then tell the other child that you have a ball you would like to share with her. Greg gets to relax and play with his ball and both children see you role model sharing.

During a game of *Puzzle Pairs* with my preschoolers, one child did not want to match her puzzle piece to her partner's piece. She refused to let go of it even to put it on the floor beside the matching piece. She began to cry when we encouraged her to hold it next to the other piece. Instead of forcing the issue, I told her very confused partner that Julie was not ready to share her piece and that we could pull out two more puzzle pieces and play a second round. Julie held her original piece for the rest of the session and the playing continued.

The lessons in all of this are to focus our attention on the children and their needs. Their actions are the clues that guide us toward understanding their needs. It is not about playing the game *right*. It's about learning from play. There are many, many ways we learn. The games you play will be more fun for you and the children if you allow for the very varied developmental needs of the children to be valued.

The Experiential Learning Cycle

Experiential learning is more than simply learning by doing. Much learning takes place when we reflect on an experience. When we step back and recall what oc-curred—events, feelings, results—we are able to highlight the specific successes and learnings from an activity. Having analyzed the experiences, we can then experiment with new ideas and behaviors in future activities.

The Experiential Learning Cycle consists of:

1) an event or activity

2) reflecting on the event, a brief discussion or processing of the activity

3) decisions to improve upon behaviors and processes in future attempts

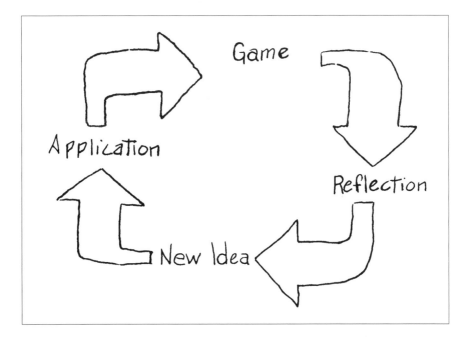

4) opportunity to grow—another activity or the same activity continued

Our challenge is to create situations in which the learning cycle is effective for the developmental abilities of both the group as a whole and the individuals in the group. Four- to eight-year-olds are quite capable of reflecting on an activity and drawing learnings from their experience. The key is that any processing of an activity must be brief and as immediate to the activity as possible.

Circling up the group so that everyone can see and hear each other is an ideal way to convey information and have a group discussion. When you can create this learning environment, DO. However, it may not always be practical. Often, the simple act of forming a circle is a ten-minute activity with new conflicts bubbling up. Who stands next to whom, who pushed whom, who touched whom, analyzing the shape of the formation. Children will drift off knowing that a not so active event is ahead … by the time the circle is formed there may be ten new issues to discuss! The activity you wanted to discuss has become ancient history. (See page 39 for tips on circling up.)

The best processing strategy is often to do it right in the middle of the activity. Try having everyone freeze where they stand. Then ask the questions, "What just happened?" "How are we doing on our safety rules?" "Is this strategy working?" "How can you solve this problem?" "How are people feeling?" You might even ask a question or make an observation and move on without any discussion at all. This could be the only processing you do with preschoolers.

With early elementary grades, I have found that a quick feelings check will reveal what is and isn't working. First and second graders are very ready to tell you what just happened. A comment such as, "We are not listening to each other," is a great lead-in to asking how that feels. The feelings are just a layer or two down and a couple of questions will get you there. Real issues that children bring up provide great opportunities for teaching problem solving. You might say to the group, "What ideas do you have that might help us listen to one another?"

After a brief discussion, quietly summarize the ideas that were decided upon. This makes the learning clear to everyone. It will assist the group in knowing what they may be working on in the next game.

Summary—Putting the Principles to Work

Creating an environment where children feel safe and comfortable is the first step towards teaching communication and cooperation skills. By using the principles of Challenge By Choice, the Full Value Contract and the Experiential Learning Cycle you will be better able to facilitate the children's learning through the activities and move toward adventure play goals:

- working with other children
- communicating, being able to express emotions and share ideas
- movement skills
- early learning about cooperation, problem solving with a group, sequencing tasks and helping one another toward a common goal
- trusting oneself and others
- solving conflicts

Chapter Two

Some Commonly Asked Questions

If using adventure with young children is new to you—whether you know adventure but don't know preschoolers and early elementary grade children, or you know the kids but don't know adventure—you probably have some questions. Some of your initial questions will be answered as you begin using the activities. Take a risk. Try some games with the children. This is where the adventure learning process begins—for the children as well as for you.

But there are also some commonly asked questions and concerns that consistently arise and to which there are some relatively simple answers and solutions. Below, in question-and-answer format, are some of the concerns that teachers indicate arise as they begin doing adventure activities with their children.

How often and for how long should we hold a games session?

As frequently as you can fit games into your schedule, do so. Games are a wonderful means of developing physical, social and conflict-resolution skills. If you play games frequently, you will notice that the children gain skill in taking care of each other through kindness, gentleness and safety.

Some teachers like to have a ritual in which they play a game to start every day or begin every recess. If I am conducting a game session as part of a weekly routine, I find that thirty minutes is a sufficient amount of time. Once in a while the children maintain interest for a longer period. At any rate, they know when they have had too much structured play and will let you know by their behavior.

What do I do when the whole group seems to be out of control, not listening and not playing safely?

Several factors could be contributing to the group's being out of control. Your first step in resolving the situation may be to identify why it's happening. The children may have been inside or involved in structured activities for too long. A structured game may be exactly what they *don't* need. The time of day may be a factor. At the end of a long day, children may have used up all their resources for listening and controlling their energy.

Read the group and help children get their needs met. Just being outside or having free-form play may be your answer. Certain groups can simply be high energy all of the time. In that case, give them what they need—lots of

running and fast-moving games. Another factor may be the number of children participating. High numbers of participants might overwhelm your students. If you have other adults, allow for a games group and a free play group. Start with smaller numbers, you'll be setting up for success.

In general, if you feel things are out of control, then they probably are. Try using a *Freeze* call to give the kids a brief time-out. Point out that things seem kind of crazy. Get their commitment to play more safely and try again. If the situation is not getting any better, then stop the activity and bring the group into a circle. Be clear that they cannot play the game if the group cannot play safely. Do not be harsh or scolding, just state your observations and allow the children to do the same. See if you can get the group to talk about why the activity was out of control. If you feel as though success can now be achieved, try again. If not, end the activity session on a reassuring note—"Let's try it again tomorrow. Let's try something else that might be easier for us to do right now."

Can I use these games with special populations?

These games and many other adventure activities can be adapted to suit children with many different physical, social and intellectual needs. Many of the activities are geared to individual achievement, and there is a wide range of choices as to how children play the game. Encourage their creativity and adaptations. This is a wonderful age to begin valuing diversity.

The Cooperative and Problem-Solving activities are structured in such a way that the group must work together to achieve a goal or solve a problem. This means that a group of diverse people, and in this case children, learn to build on the strengths of each person in the group. Very young children will do this with unabashed confidence—easily identifying what they can and cannot do. The positive side to this is the honesty with which they will speak their understanding of each other. The negative side is that their understanding of each other may not be accurate and once expressed can be hurtful. The key is to watch closely as the group learns to work together. Help them learn what it means to play kindly and safely. Teach them how to be honest with each other without hurting anyone's feelings. By doing this you are setting a strong example and helping them to see the worth of each child in the group.

Forming a circle for certain games and for discussions is very time consuming, even for seven-year-olds. Is it better not to bother trying or is there a way to do it quickly?

Circling up is a challenging task for children in this age group. During the process of forming a circle, conflicts often develop and feelings get hurt. Your original reason for circling up will be forgotten and you are now faced with a whole new set of issues. But circles are an important part of adventure play. Children are learning to work as a group and to talk with each other respectfully. The circle is the shape that allows everyone to have a place and to see each other.

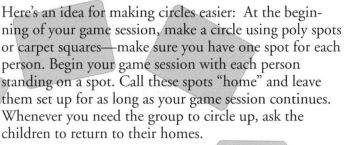

Here's an idea for making circles easier: At the beginning of your game session, make a circle using poly spots or carpet squares—make sure you have one spot for each person. Begin your game session with each person standing on a spot. Call these spots "home" and leave them set up for as long as your game session continues. Whenever you need the group to circle up, ask the children to return to their homes.

Some children will need to identify one spot as their very own, by color or number, to avoid arguments about whose spot is whose. If you have enough spots available, consider having children tape their names to a spot and then use these spots throughout the year. The other advantage of using these home spots is that they keep the kids relatively still—children are focused on staying in a small area rather than rolling or walking around.

In situations where you haven't created a home circle, you might want to convey information or conduct a process session by having everyone freeze and listen. Or try a "huddle up," which creates a tight cluster of children rather than a more structured circle. Just watch for pushing and shoving.

My game bag can be a major distraction. As soon as the children see the bag, they want to tear into it. Then they lose focus on the game at hand. What is the best way to deal with this?

The obvious answer is to take out only the equipment you need for that game session. However, this is not always the best solution if you like to be spontaneous and respond to the creativity of the children. Group momentum often takes a game session in unplanned directions. Also, group energy and dynamics are sometimes unpredictable. It's good to be prepared with a wide range of game ideas as well as props. Try getting a bag that zips up so that its contents are hidden until the time of play, or cover your props with a sheet until you are ready to use them.

You can also take cues from the children—they obviously love your toys. Remember the old motto, "If you can't beat them, join them?" Use the novelty factor to your advantage; anything new or not seen recently is exciting. Make your game bag an event in itself—open it up and allow children to play with whatever they want (except the ropes, which become safety hazards as soon as they come out of your bag). Introduce play guidelines around this activity and remind the children to Be Gentle, Be Kind and Be Safe. Watch their spontaneous play and learn from them. The children may very well create a whole new games repertoire for you.

I find that the level of safety in any game diminishes as the game continues, even though I have given clear guidelines. What can I do to help my students Be Safe?

In the excitement of a game, it is understandable that some of the rules are forgotten. When you see a safety factor being compromised, call a time-out or a Freeze. Remind children of their Full Value Contract and provide a visual demonstration of the activity's safety guidelines again. As the game continues, give feedback to the children who are working within the safety rules—"Great job with Bumpers Up, Jim!" This serves as a positive reminder of the safety rules in the midst of the action.

If safety has disintegrated beyond repair, it may be a signal to change gears completely and play a sit-down game.

Remember that the successful completion of the game is not the goal here. You are using play activities to help children learn. So, if a game doesn't go so well, that's

OK. Use the situation as a teachable moment. "Why did we stop playing?" "What could we do to make the game more fun, more safe, more fair?" "What will you do differently if we try playing again?"

Do not become frustrated or disappointed in the children. Remind them, and yourself, that this is all about learning. Sometimes learning means we make mistakes. Mistakes can be very helpful. They show us what doesn't work and encourage us to think about what does work. If you can play by this philosophy, you'll be helping these young children open their minds to trying, knowing that trying doesn't always mean you do it right.

I have several children who never participate in games. I don't force them to play, but just how far do you go with the Challenge by Choice philosophy?

Let them "not participate." Remember, some children need to observe, even from a distance, before they feel ready to join the group. Certainly you can set guidelines for what they can do instead, but requiring them to play when they do not feel ready will only add to their discomfort. If these children develop negative attitudes about the games, it may intimidate the children who do choose to play. Allowing the reluctant children to step back and observe until they choose to play is better for everyone.

At the same time, don't give up on them. Try to find a game or challenge that draws them in, such as *Can You?* or *Beep, Time's Up.* Enlisting them as helpers works well, too. Sometimes children need a personal connection to feel comfortable playing. You can take on this role.

What you don't want to have happen is seven children playing while three children run wild in the classroom. Make it clear—"You don't have to play, but if you don't I would like you to sit here, help me monitor the game, go to the reading area or…" Provide options that are safe and comfortable for you and for the children.

What do I do when two children have a conflict in the middle of a game? Frequently, children push each other or have a tug-of-war over certain props. Should I stop the game or continue on and talk to those children later?

The answer goes back to the question, "What are your goals for this game session?" For me, the game is not the ultimate reason for playing. Creating a safe and trusting environment is a very important reason for playing. When conflict occurs, it needs to be effectively addressed.

The children involved need your support in working through the conflict, but equally important, the other children who witness the conflict need to know you will attend to it. They are taking mental notes on how the situation is resolved. They will feel safer knowing that when and if they are in a similar situation, they will get what they need. Time-outs, comments such as "use your words," and your suggested solutions have only short-term impact. The children don't learn tools for resolving conflict when these strategies are employed.

Diane Levin's book *Teaching Young Children in Violent Times,* published by Educators for Social Responsibility, is a good resource for how to work through conflicts. Her four-step process is useful here:

1. Define the problem but do not assess blame. Acknowledge both children's point of view as legitimate.
2. Find a solution to which they both can agree. Allow them to share their ideas and involve them in the decision making.
3. Help them put their agreed upon solution into practice.
4. Reflect back with them on how they feel it worked. All of this process helps children develop skills for living.

I would add that you should use your judgment as to how you go about conducting the above process. If you have several teachers available, you might want to work with the two children alone while the game continues. If you are by yourself, you may want to involve the entire group in working on the issue. The time you spend constructively resolving these conflicts will pay off when future conflicts arise.

My students always want to play the same game. They are so disappointed when I introduce a new game. How can I help them open up to games we haven't played before?

Young children need and enjoy repetition. It helps them learn a game, develop specific skills and gives them self-confidence. If a group is very enthusiastic about playing a particular game, I go ahead and play it. You might want to start your session with this game and then move on to a different game. Older children can often hold off and play new games knowing that you will get to their game before the end of the session.

Figure out what it is about the game they like so much and find a game that has that same component. For example, if it's the running they love, try another running game.

How do you know when a game is not a positive experience? We played a game of Run Rabbit Run on our playground. Children joined us as we played, but in spite of the game being attractive to many children, something didn't feel quite right.

This is an important question. Games can be tools for building cooperation, communication, problem-solving and other skills as well as for exercising the body. But simply playing games does not necessarily bring about positive results. Unless you are careful, games can even be a negative experience for some children. Generally, I assess the situation with two questions:

1. Is this game helping the group meet the goals we have established? For example: Is the group working together? Developing communication skills? Burning some energy? Exercising problem-solving skills?

2. Is the Full Value Contract being attended to: Be Gentle, Be Safe and Be Kind?

If you can answer yes to both of these questions, the game is probably a positive experience for the children.

I've tried partnering games with five-year-olds, but it takes so much work to get them to pair up. Are they just not ready for these activities?

Never give up on an activity because it failed once. Back up and analyze what happened. Can you break the game down into smaller increments? What skills can you work on to help the children gain success at playing the game? Examine the game from all angles—social, emotional, cognitive and physical.

Children are not generally being mean when they refuse a partner, although we often interpret it that way. Partnering is a skill that evolves as children develop trust in others. Children do what feels safe to them. They choose to pair up with children they feel safe with. Try less threatening partnering games like *Categories, Puzzle*

Pairs and People to People, and slowly work your way to more challenging pair activities such as *Sticky Buddies* or *Trust Walk.*

I have a hard time getting my groups to listen to the ground rules of a game or have a discussion about problem solving.

Ask yourself what need are the children expressing through their non-attentive behavior? Young children love to run. Any running game seems to capture both their spirit and interest. It is the reverse of what works with older children and adults. If I start a games session with a high-energy game such as *Beep, Time's Up* or *Fox in the Morning,* I have much more success with the problem-solving and trust activities that follow. In fact, before I circle up the group to lay the ground rules of the session and check in with the children, I need to do one of these games.

As for problem-solving opportunities, you may not always have the full attention of the entire group. Focus on a small cluster of children or even just one or two children to help them gain problem-solving skills. Taking the time to circle up a group to have a discussion is not always effective. Use your judgment as to when to pull the large group together in a circle or freeze.

If the group is hearing the ground rules but is not able to follow through on them, you might be asking too much on both a physical and cognitive level. Sometimes when children are playing a game "incorrectly," they reveal to us a variation of the game that better meets their needs for fun and creativity.

I'm concerned about doing blindfold games with my children. It just doesn't seem like a safe thing to do.

Blindfold games or close-your-eyes games are extremely challenging for this age group. Your concern for safety is justified. Many teachers prefer only using the eyes-closed option, eliminating all use of blindfolds. This method allows "peeking by choice" so that individuals can challenge themselves according to their readiness. You might find that peeking is the norm for almost the entire game. If this is the case, you may wonder if you should

even bother. However, remember that growth comes in very small increments. Each time children choose to close their eyes, they are challenging themselves to grow in their way and on their own terms.

If you experiment with eyes-closed activities, start off in a controlled way where only two children are playing and you are very present as a spotter and coach. Start with the easiest variation and work up to the more difficult ones so that you have a clear picture of the children's readiness for the responsibility of taking care of each other. The benefits of trust-building activities are enormous, but if not done safely, they can quickly break down any trust that exists. It is extremely difficult to repair a child's trust in others once lost, so choose these activities only when you can closely supervise them.

Summary

Adventure activities offer tremendous opportunities for learning for both teachers and children. It is our belief that the best learning takes place experientially—by doing something, reflecting on it and trying again. This is the model we recommend for you. When you have questions, identify and clarify your concerns, develop your own solutions and test them out. Don't be afraid to make mistakes or play games that don't work so well. The goal is to learn, and there is something to learn from every experience.

How children will react to any activity is not always predictable. But if you set a tone of safety reminding the children to Be Gentle, Be Kind and Be Safe, you will soon find that the play experiences are meaningful and fun.

Chapter Three

Planning An Adventure Play Program

In the development of this book, I was lucky enough to be invited into many preschools and after-school programs. Often, I would visit programs once or twice a week as a guest or enrichment teacher. The children

rarely remembered my name but pretty consistently, in every school, they dubbed me "The Game Lady." I found it quite flattering to be associated with their fun and games experiences.

I found a rhythm with the games that I think you can use, too. There are some games that work really well together. Below are some of the ideas I have found to work when planning a games session, as well as specific recommendations for a five-session plan.

Timing

I recommend a session of about one hour. Some of that time will be active games playing, some sit-down or other activities, like making your own props.

In my experience, 30 to 40 minutes of straight games playing is about the maximum amount of time that preschoolers and kindergartners can maintain energy and interest. You can stretch that time frame with older children, as always, depending on the size and personality of your group. Some days ten minutes is all they can handle. Be ready for that.

The beauty of programs that are an hour or longer is that you can do more than just play games. First, you can ease into the session, taking time to allow the children to fully transition from the preceding events of their day. Whether snack, naps, art, music or math occur before a games playing session, they need time to adjust to the new activity. Ask some opening questions—"Do you remember the games we played last time?" "What were they?" "What are your favorite games?"

Second, you can plan activities that involve children in creating their own play items. This is an important part of the adventure. Store-bought, one-game-only toys are not necessary for play. Children become a part of the whole play experience by creating the toys and then creating the games that they can play with those toys. Remember making paper airplanes, using rocks, sticks and shirts for kickball bases, crushing soda cans to make a heel for your shoe, building forts out of whatever you could find? We can foster this sort of ingenuity about playing with today's children.

Creating toys can bring out dimensions of children that you might not notice as you play games. I vividly remember the day I sat with one group painting bean bags. I learned about their families, their passions, their sense of humor. One very quiet boy talked more to me during that activity than any other time during my games program. The connections formed on that day were rich. It was a turning point for me and my relationship with those children.

Creating a play item also serves the purpose of bridging the child's games experience from school to home. The adventure they began with you can continue at home with Mom, Dad, siblings and friends.

Sample Program

An adventure play program consists of games, group problem-solving initiatives, and trust-building activities. Children are encouraged to work and play together rather than compete against one another. Through these playful activities and discussions, children learn how to communicate their ideas and feelings to one another. "Be Gentle, Be Kind, Be Safe" are the three guidelines we use to help create an environment that is emotionally and physically safe as well as challenging and fun.

The following sample five-session program is based on an enrichment program I facilitated with preschool-aged children. As you well know, every plan is subject to the unpredictable needs and whims of your group. I can almost guarantee that you will not play all the games you put into your lesson plan. The group will be totally engrossed in one game twice as long as you expect or they will have a burning desire to play a game from the previous week. Each session becomes truly an Adventure.

Structure

1 1/2 hours each session

12 to 15 students

Program Goals

- To foster a sense of gentleness and kindness among the children.

- To play games that require children to work on challenges cooperatively, both with one other child and with the group as a whole.

- To give children an opportunity to create play items or "toys" as well as to foster their creativity by allowing them to "invent games."

- To encourage children to express their ideas and feelings as they arise in our activities.

Session One

Goals

- To begin to understand the meaning of Be Gentle, Be Kind, Be Safe.
- To establish the beginnings of trust at the group level.

Activities

Set up a circle using poly spots (one spot for each child).

Ask each child to take a "spot" in the circle and sit down. Begin by talking a little about this new project called Adventure Play. Tell the children that they will be playing games, working together and having fun. "While we are playing we will also be learning to Be Gentle, Be Kind, Be Safe…" Continue with a brief introduction to each of these concepts. Then briefly discuss Challenge by Choice. (Refer back to Chapter One.)

Now it's time to play some games…

Name Game (even if they already know each other)

Red-Handed

All Aboard

Can You

Trust Circle with *Triangle, Circle, Square Variation*

Beep, Times up

Making Bean Bags

Once you think the children have had enough activity, move into the bean bag making project. Show the group a sample of homemade bean bags. Discuss the procedures for making their own bean bags. "Today we'll decorate our bags using paints and markers. Next week, we'll fill and finish the bags and use them for some games."

Materials Needed

> √ white cloth—two 5" by 5" squares for each child
> √ fabric paints
> √ permanent markers
> √ masking tape to hold cloth flat on table
> √ poly spots—one for each child

Prep

Pre-cut the 5" by 5" squares of fabric.

Have a large table ready with the squares taped down to the table. This will help keep the cloth from slipping around while the children decorate. Place the tape about 1/2" onto each side of the square. This allows the children to paint only on the surfaces that will show once the bag is sewn together. It can be very upsetting to have your face, cats legs or sun partially cut off in the final product.

Decorate bean bag cloths with fabric paints and markers. Once everyone is finished, put the bags in a safe place to dry.

Closing

Have children go back to their home spots for a wrap-up discussion. End with *The Coming and Going of the Rain.*

Session Two

Goals

- Completion of bean bags
- To foster children's ability to create games with their bean bags.
- To continue developing skills for trusting one another and taking care of one another.

Finishing the Bean Bags

After the paint has dried on the childrens' bean bags, sew 1/2" seams on all but two inches of each bean bag. Be sure the decorated sides are facing each other so the seams end up on the inside of the bags. After sewing, turn the bags right side out, ready to be filled by the children.

Materials Needed

√ wide funnels

√ beans or rice

√ needle and thread

Steps

Fill bean bags with beans. Children can fill their own bags with some assistance if needed. Then close up the bean bags with final stitches (helpers are nice if you want to speed up the process and get into playing with the bags right away).

Now its time to play some games with the newly created bean bags.

Start with the childrens' ideas for games to play with their bean bags. Encourage their creativity by playing some of their game ideas. Work with the children to rethink ideas that might not be manageable or safe.

Activities

Try some of these with the bean bags:

Bean Bag Balance

Obstacle Course with bean bag balance

Pairs Tag and with bean bag

Bocci and Vertical Bocci

Bean Bag Treasure Hunt

If you think your children are ready, try doing the trust activity *Sleepy Snakes*.

Closing

Wrap up the discussion at home spots and repeat *Red Handed* from Session One.

Session Three

Goals

- Continue to build on the children's understanding of "Be Gentle, Be Kind, Be Safe."
- Develop skills for cooperating and communicating with a partner.

Set up your home circle using poly spots.

Begin with children at their home spots. Talk about the games you played last session. Remind the children of being gentle, kind, and safe. Ask them to give you examples of each.

Making Trash Balls

Materials Needed

√ old newspapers (5–6 pieces per child)
√ masking tape
√ markers

Prep

Have a table area set up for the children to make trashballs.

"Today we'll be making large balls using pieces of newspaper and masking tape." Take a two-page piece of newspaper and loosely ball it up. Wrap a second piece around it. Then wrap masking tape randomly around the ball, just enough to hold the ball together. The children can do most of this job. If they need assistance, it is usually with the taping. Have markers available to decorate or put their name on their own trash ball.

Activities

Once the balls are done, return to your home circle. Begin by asking the children for ideas of games they would like to play with trash balls. Try a couple of the ideas. Then move on to these games:

Chaotic Team Juggle with Trash Balls

Group Juggle (for older children)

Help Me or Else or *Buddy Help Me or Else*

Catch Up—Quail Shooters Delight

Trash Ball Bocci

Trust activities

Sticky Buddies

Buddy games:

Rolling Toe to Toe or *Maple Syrup Pull-Up*

Session Four

Goals

- To continue developing skills for working with a buddy.

Begin as usual in your home circle (or, for some variety, with everyone sitting on a rug). Review what you did together in the last game session. Talk briefly about being safe and gentle and kind.

Making Milk Jug Catchers

"Today we'll be making jugs using milk containers. The containers are already cut and ready to use once we decorate them." Give the children some supplies to use in decorating and allow 15–20 minutes for them to work.

Materials Needed

 √ one milk container (plastic one-gallon type) per
 child

 √ stickers, other supplies appropriate for decorating
 plastic

Prep

Have the children bring in empty (and rinsed) gallon
size plastic milk containers the week before you plan on
using them. Your job is to cut off the bottom of each
container so that it is now more like a scoop.

Prepare an area for decorating the jugs.

Steps

When their decorating is completed, regroup on the rug
or in a circle. Ask the children how they might play with
these new toys. Once you've gotten some of their ideas,
try them. Then try these games:

> *Scooping and Pouring* or *Scooping and Pouring
> Relay* (see Milk Jug Games)
>
> *Help Me or Else* using milk jugs (see variation)
>
> *Buddy Rolling* and *Tossing with Catchers*
>
> *Puzzle Pairs*
>
> *People to People*
>
> *Sticky Buddy* review
>
> *Obstacle Course*

Session Five

Goals

- To build on the cooperation skills that children
  are developing.
- To give children opportunities to express their
  ideas in group problem-solving situations.

- To encourage expressions of feelings within or after activities.

Begin with your group in their home circle. Review games and learning from previous sessions.

Making Mesh Scarves

Materials Needed

√ squares of mesh fabric in approximately 15" by 15" pieces, one for each child

√ good fabric scissors if you are going to let the children cut their own. (Hold the fabric taut while they do the cutting.)

Prep

If your group is too young to be cutting fabric, pre-cut the scarves into 15" by 15" squares.

Steps

Demonstrate how to cut the mesh fabric. Review scissors safety and require an adult to hold the fabric taut while the children cut it.

When the children have finished cutting the fabric into scarves, play some games with them.

Feathers and Scarves and variations

Quick Line Up (use different color scarves for front, back, and sides)

Marshmallow River (use scarves as the marshmallows)

The Clock

Closing

Wrap-up discussion: since this is the last session, review with the children the games played, the props they made, and some of the learning highlights. Encourage them to keep creating their own games and toys and remember to *Be Gentle, Be Kind, Be Safe.*

Chapter Four

Bag Of Tricks

Half the fun of playing games with kids is accumulating your props. Game items can be found just about anywhere—from your basement, to school storage closets, to fabric stores, pet supply stores, craft stores, garage sales and, of course, toy stores. There are catalogues that specialize in teaching materials for physical education and recreation programs and if you have the budget, by all means get the good stuff. However, if you don't have the money, most of the props you need for the games in this book can be made or purchased for pennies.

Ideas

Beach balls—all sizes

Bean bags (refer back to Chapter Three to make your own)

Rubber spots (pie plates painted bright colors are good substitutes)

Carpet squares (remnants)

Spots in various shapes, circles, squares, hearts, trains, etc.

Old ropes—the bigger the diameter the better. Old climbing rope works well. Old hawser laid rope is fantastic. Have various lengths ready for different games.

Safety Note +

Only let children play with ropes under your supervision. Ropes turned into whips can do damage physically and quickly undermine feelings of trust you are trying to build.

Sponge balls

Fleece balls

Shaker noise makers (easily home made)

Cones for boundary markers

Deck rings

Rubber chickens

Large dice

Masking tape

Blanket or sheet

Hoops, both small and large

Cardboard boxes—for tunnels, hiding, sitting in, pushing…

Chalk

Bandannas for blindfolds, connecting buddies, balancing on heads

Stuffed animals

Puppets

Spandex or lycra fabric

Scarves—light weight and silk are the coolest

Items Easily Made

Shakers—fill small hand-size plastic containers with rice, beans or popcorn. Tape the cover closed with duct tape or masking tape and decorate.

Milk Jug Catchers—Cut half-gallon plastic milk jugs half way down horizontally. Leave enough of a scoop to catch a medium-sized ball as you hold the handle. Half gallon jugs are good for younger children and rolling and passing games rather than throwing and catching.

Cardboard Box Tunnels—Line up a series of boxes that have the bottoms cut out of them. Make a project of painting them and then include the tunnels in an obstacle course activity or simply as forts or caves.

Polyfiber Filled Balls—Buy nylons or use old ones and a bag of polyfiber, used to make stuffed animals. Knot one end of the nylons and stuff it with enough polyfiber to make the size ball you want. Cut nylons leaving enough room to put a knot in that end. You can get fancy and dye the nylons bright colors, or draw designs on white ones. I can usually get about eight various sized balls out of one pair of nylons. The price is definitely right and if you really pack in the polyfiber, you will get nearly the same result in throwability as a fleece ball—for about a tenth the cost.

Polyfiber Comet Balls—Fill the nylon as above but leave a tail about eight to twelve inches and tie a third knot. Knee highs make great *Comet Balls* as they are the right length without cutting. The resulting balls with a tail are fun spinning and throwing objects.

Puzzle Pairs Pieces—Buy foam board at an art store (about $2.00 a sheet) and cut our your puzzle pieces with a razor knife. I made squares first then cut them into two pieces. The edges can get frayed as you cut but the end result is a nice thick piece of board that is relatively durable and works well for the puzzle games.

Spandex Fabric Tubes—Buy a minimum of five yards of spandex in bright colors. For toddler games, I cut the 40" width in half. I left one of these pieces in its full length. The other I cut into two sections of 2 1/2 feet each. I made these into tubes by simply sewing the ends together. Fabric tubes can be used with three of four children inside stretching out the fabric and testing its springiness. The larger piece can be used with a group of eight or ten children inside. If you might be playing spandex games with older children or even adults, you will want to keep the spandex in the full 40" width. Experiment with different size tubes.

Buddy Ropes—Cut old climbing rope, 9mm or 11 mm into 2-foot lengths to use for *Letter Making* or *Buddy Walks*. They also make great jump ropes.

Inside Outside, Upside Down Hoop Triangle—Use three hoops to create a triangular "house." Use masking tape to attach the hoops together. If you have hoops of different colors use three different colors.

Trash Balls—Take two or three large, double pages of newspaper and roll them into a ball. Then wrap masking tape around the outside just enough to keep a somewhat round shape. Decorate them if you want. At a minimum, put childrens' names on their balls. It's very important to many children to know which ball is their own and always nice to take home a toy.

Your Game Bag

If you are trying to play a specific game, having your open game bag in sight will be a major distraction to one child, then two, then three and finally the bag itself will become the game. Have a sheet to put over it or keep it out of sight until you're ready to move on to a new game.

If you do not have a particular game in mind, simply pulling out the game bag generates all kinds of creativity. You'll see your "toys" being used in ways you never thought of or read about in any game book. This may trigger ideas that you can try on the spot or save for another time.

For safety reasons you'll need to monitor this free-form activity closely. I recommend keeping any ropes and string you have away from the children. Even under close supervision these items very quickly can become harmful.

Section Two

Activities

Introduction

Most of the games in this book are variations of games you may have seen in other books. I have kept the more commonly known names of the games so that you may recall the original game and have an idea of its basic concept. Sometimes, the adaptation described is not a great deal different from the original. Others are markedly different. As you read each game description, don't

stop at the first description before you decide that it is appropriate or inappropriate for your group.

The variations that follow may be easier or more challenging and are often different enough that you will find that at least one of them is appropriate for your group. Each game description provides you with Space and Prop requirements. Definitions of the Space descriptors are the minimum requirement necessary.

Small: Any indoor classroom without a great deal of open floor space will work for these games.

Medium: Indoor spaces such as classrooms that have an open floor plan or in which the furniture has been moved aside are appropriate for games with this description.

Large/Open: A gym or outdoor setting with plenty of room to run and throw things are required for these games.

You will notice that no descriptor is given for group size. The reason for this is that just about every game can be played with two or twenty children without any alteration of the game as described. Occasionally a game will work better with a minimum number of players. If this is the case it is noted within the Set Up specifics.

Safety Notes

There is much to be aware of when working with young children—what they are touching, how they are using a toy, how they are playing with others. Because of this, the best strategy for maintaining safety is prevention. We have found that spending time on how we play together using the Full Value Contract (refer back to Chapter One) is a great prevention tool. If you all have a common language, "Hey, let's play safe!" then prevention becomes a lot easier.

There are some common issues that typically arise when using Adventure Play. Below is a brief summary of some of the issues we have run into.

Balloons

Although many game resource books include balloon games, we have intentionally omitted them from this book. Balloons are a choking hazard when deflated or popped. Many preschools and elementary schools have banned balloons from their properties to avoid any related risk. We recommend that when working with young populations you find substitutes for balloons. Beach balls and sponge balls, scarves and feathers seem to fill the gap quite well.

Bumpers Up

In any walking or running activity, foreheads and noses have the potential to collide. To prevent accidents, use the Bumpers Up position. Hands are in front of the face, elbows are bent. Demonstrate the position and have everyone practice it before entering into a fast moving, congested tag game.

Tug of War

When children see a rope they usually think it is for playing tug of war. I am never comfortable with tug of war, even in highly supervised situations. The potential for injury is very high, and it is counterproductive to the goals of establishing a sense of trust, safety and coopera- tion. The war is usually a harsh lesson in We Win, You Lose. When I tell children that we won't be playing play tug of war, I show them how a rope could slide through their hands giving them a painful rope burn. I also show them how one or both persons could be pulled to the ground. Then I move on and show them how we can use the rope so that everyone can have fun.

Hoops

Hoops are great fun for free play and for structured games. But only use them when you can closely super- vise the group. Children love to get inside hoops to-

gether and walk around as a team! Be aware of their speed when doing this and be ready as a spotter to help them if they lose balance. Also, keep the hoop from riding up to their necks for obvious reasons. If you are using the hoops that come in sections be-  ware— they tend to become weapons when they come apart.

Ropes

Use ropes of any kind or length only with the greatest supervision. Once rope becomes wrapped around an arm, leg or waist, not to mention neck, the danger factor is too high. When I let children play with my game bag, I often hold onto the ropes, saving them for the structured games.

Balls

There is really no need to have balls that are harder or heavier than fleece or sponge balls. Both types have enough weight so that they can be thrown quite a distance. Trash balls can be made large enough to be caught by even the youngest players. (See Chapter Three for directions on making trash balls.)

Freeze

Teach your children how to freeze as quickly as they can upon hearing the command. It is a valuable tool to use when an activity is headed in an unsafe direction.

Practice First

Providing a visual demonstration of how to play a game goes a long way in preventing injuries. Demonstrate direction of travel, bumpers up, staying inside the boundaries, tagging methods, walking vs. running, etc. Sometimes, you just need to play to understand. In these cases play a practice round of the game—go slower than you'll actually play and only play for a minute or two.

Chapter Five

Body Skills, Stretches and Warm-Ups

Warm-Ups are always a good way to begin an Adventure Play session. Muscles, bones, hearts and lungs need to wake up gradually. Although this is more critical for

adults, children do well when they are allowed to ease into a new situation and transition to new activities.

The games and activities in this chapter tend to focus on individual skills more than team skills. I have found them to be helpful in focusing the children

on fun and adventure without intimidating or overwhelming them. Children who need to assess the situation can do so and join in when they feel safe and comfortable.

Teaching Children to Cheer for One Another

Try this as a goal for one of your games to develop children's abilities to give each other positive feedback. Play *Over the River* and allow children to jump over the river alone or in pairs. The rest of the group watches and says something positive to the jumpers—

"Good jump Bobby!"

"Nice job Sue!"

"You're strong Katherine!"

The cheering will slow the activity down in a nice way. It may feel contrived at first, but that's OK. Developing the language of kindness is a skill that needs focused practice.

Giving children the skills to express their feelings helps them learn to value themselves as well as others. Every activity has a potential to bring up a variety of feelings. As you identify children's feelings, you can help them to recognize those feelings and know that it is OK to feel them. "Are you frustrated about having a hard time with this? Would you like some help from one of the other children or me?" "Are you sad about Jane not letting you join in? That doesn't seem very kind does it? Jane, did you know Sam is sad about not being able to join you in this activity?" One of our roles as teachers is to facilitate the expression of feelings, acknowledge them, value them, and to help children to recognize and value their own feelings and those of others.

I See

This game challenges children's abilities to follow directions. It is flexible enough that you can play in a cramped classroom or on a wide open filed. Try gradually increasing the number of tasks. The tasks can vary according to how much space you have and how active you want the group to be.

Space   Small

Props   None

How to Play

Say to the group, "I see children touching their toes." Begin to act out what you say. Move quickly to the next challenge: "I see everyone hopping to the slide." Rapidly moving from one task to the next gives the group a sense of urgency in trying to complete each one quickly. Mix in commands that require the children to do more dramatic play.

"I see trees swaying in the wind."

"I see race car drivers heading down the field."

"I see dogs scratching their ears, and rolling on the ground."

Ideas for active commands:

I see children—

...doing the crab walk

...skipping to the door

...chasing me

...running to the tree

Ideas for smaller spaces:

I see children—

...touching something red

...touching their noses

...children with their feet in the air

...touching a square

...snapping fingers (or clapping hands)

...with hands in the air

...sitting with legs crossed

...with rabbit ears

...with raccoon eyes

...with whiskers

Ideas for group interaction:

I see children—

...touching someone's toes, nose, shoulder

...shaking hands

...doing the leap frog

...linking elbows with a buddy

...making a triangle with their bodies

...creating the letter T with another person

...sitting in a circle

Very Active:

I see—

...birds flying in the sky

...rabbits jumping up and down

…trees swaying in the wind

…race car drivers

…doggies scratching their ears, and rolling on the ground

…children running across the field

…children rolling like a log

…children somersaulting

Tip

Try this as a transition activity, ending with whatever it is you want the children to be doing next. "I see children standing in a line at the door, ready to go outside…"

Can You...?

I love to start a game session with *Can You...?* It draws in the child who is shy or nervous and helps capture the attention of the children who are cautious or drifting away. Everyone likes to show off what they can do. And children love to practice a fun challenge they can't yet perform.

Space Cozy

Props None

How to Play

Start off giving the group a *Can You...?* that you know all of the children can do. Gradually add to the level of difficulty and creativity. Recognize children who can do the task with a "Good job." "Nice hopping." or "You did it!" Also reward children who are working hard to master a skill or try something new. "You're almost there." and "Try again, you've almost got it." "You are very focused!" Encourage the children to support one another and cheer each other on.

Can You—

> ...balance on both knees and both hands
>
> ...balance on knees and one hand... just knees... one knee
>
> ...do the crab walk
>
> ...crab walk with a bean bag on your belly

Skills to try while sitting down:

> ...snap your fingers
>
> ...whistle

...make a peace sign

...cross your fingers

...make a loon call cupping your hands and blowing into them

...wink

...raise an eye brow

...cluck your tongue

...make a "pop" sound putting your index finger into your mouth and pulling out against your cheek

...make raccoons eyes (put your thumb and fore finger into a circle, turn them upside down with your fingers pointing down and place the circles over your eyes)

Active skills:

...hop on one foot

...do a somersault

...jump and click your heels

...lock elbows with a buddy and run to a destination

...walk backwards to a destination

...jump over a small obstacle

...do the egg roll—lie on your back and grab your knees, pulling them close into your body. Then roll back and forth like an egg would.

Tips

Have children add their own *Can You?* to the list. Think about your group, modify and add to this list. This is a game that children enjoy playing over and over. Try using it to reinforce skills you are teaching. For example, "Can you count to ten? Can you do it backwards? Can you tie your shoe?"

Windmill and Popcorn

These body skill activities add the challenge of working with a buddy. *Windmill* and *Popcorn* are almost a dance, so add music to the scene after the children have mastered the challenge. You may have to demonstrate these movements a few times and actively coach the children until they become comfortable with the movements.

Props   None

Space   Small

Windmill

How to Play

In pairs, have the children hold hands while standing face to face. Tell them that they have the power to make it windy by creating a windmill with their partner. While holding hands (and not letting go), the pairs twist slowly away from each other. This will cause one set of arms to go up and over their heads, with the other arms following, allowing them to turn all the way around. Partners can windmill once, going slowly at first and gradually adding a little more speed and a few turns. Remind children to be gentle.

Windmill is more challenging than meets the eye, especially for four- and five-year-olds. For these children, one spin may be difficult enough, even with coaching. Children who accomplish *Windmill* may be ready for *Popcorn*.

Popcorn

How to Play

Stand back to back with a partner. With your arms hanging straight down at your sides, hands flat with your palms facing forward, reach back and place your palms—with your palms still facing forward—against your partner's palms. Bring your (both partners) arms from one side up and over your head, remaining palm to palm with your partner, all the way around to your waists. The other hands then come up and move inside the other hands and go down to touch the ground. It's not really as complicated as it sounds here. Try it a few times before you demonstrate for the children.

Safety Note +

Both *Windmill* and *Popcorn* should be avoided by anyone with back or shoulder problems. This is not usually a concern for children but might be for parents and teachers.

The Dog Stretch

The true master of this game and maybe the creator of the *Dog Stretch* is long time Project Adventure staffer Jim Schoel. I cannot do this stretch without thinking of him and his most accurate and comical imitation of a dog waking up.

Space   Cozy

Props   None

How to Play

I usually introduce this stretch by asking the group if anyone has a dog. "What do they look like when they sleep? Do they twitch? What do they do as they wake up?" Their responses tend to loosen us up and lend lightness and humor to the moment. These are the best conditions for having fun with this activity.

Tell the children you are going to wake up your whole body the very same way a dog wakes up.

Begin to move parts of your body, one at a time, starting with your eye brows, then your nose, mouth, neck. Keep working your way down your body. Once a body part is in motion continue moving it and stay with it for a while before putting another body part into motion.

It doesn't take long for everyone to feel very silly and completely woken up.

Hoop Tunnel

Children love to play in tunnels and forts. *Hoop Tunnel* builds on this inclination. Using children to help hold up the hula hoops, they make a tunnel to pass through. I once tried throwing a blanket over the hoops to enclose it and make it more tunnel-like, but in doing so lost my ability to offer guidance, instruction and supervision. Simplicity works best. Stick with the hoops.

Space   Small

Props   Two to ten hula hoops

How to Play

Stand two hoops, more if you have helpers, vertically on the floor creating a tunnel effect. If you've got a lot of hoops, partner children up and give one hoop to each twosome. Have the partners hold the hoops and create a line of hoops for an extra-long tunnel.

For three- and four-year-olds, simply crawling through the tunnel is engaging enough.

To add to the challenge have two children go through together first in the same direction then in opposite directions.

The more physically agile children can try to crawl through the tunnel without touching the hoops.

Variation

Hoop Tunnel Tag

Have group members hold as many hoops as they can to create a long tunnel. Two children play tag. The *It* child starts at one end of the tunnel and the *Chasee* starts just inside the tunnel. On *GO* the It child crawls outside the tunnel toward the entrance, while the Chassee crawls through the tunnel to the exit and along the outside of the tunnel back to the entrance. Play continues until It catches Chasee OR until you yell *SWITCH*. At that point the two children reverse their roles or let another twosome play.

Inside, Outside, Upside Down

Following directions, understanding spatial relationships and differentiating color are all possible learnings from this game. You'll see the children's ability to comprehend and follow-through with your instructions grow the more you play it.

Space   Small

Props   Hula hoops of different colors and masking tape

How to Play

Tape three different colored hoops together to make a sort of triangular house. Make several houses so that more than one child can play at a time. If you form small groups, children can watch others, support them and learn as they watch.

Some possible instructions from easiest to more challenging:

…Go into the house.

…Put your feet through the red hoop.

...Hold the house over your head. Walk around the house.

...Go inside the house through the red hoop.

...Go out through the green hoop.

...Reach through the house and touch hands with someone in your group.

...Put your feet through the blue hoop.

...Jump out of the house over the green hoop.

...Go into the house leading with one part of your body and leave leading with a different body part.

...Go through each hoop backwards.

Mirror

This classic Project Adventure cooperative activity has people working in pairs. With four- to eight-year-olds it works best with one leader and everyone else mirroring their actions. Slow motion movements can help unwind an active group, while high energy movements can give children a real aerobic experience.

Space   Small

Props   None

How to Play

Face your group and ask them to spread out so that their arms can move in any direction without touching anyone.

Invite the children to do what you do.

Be creative with your movements. Mirror is a wonderful tool that can be used to give your group whatever they need... slow motion stretches, goofy faces and positions, or high energy running and jumping.

Have children take turns being the lead person, but you may need to coach them at this at least to begin.

Twizzle

This is a consistent crowd pleaser, providing plenty of exercise for our laugh muscles. Children always have ideas to add to the list of commands, so, once played, *Twizzle* is never the same again. Let your (and their) creativity take over!

Space   Medium

Props   None

How to Play

The object of *Twizzle* is to have fun while following a set of commands and freezing as quickly as you can. The leader—you, at first—will give any one of the following commands and in any order:

WALK—Everyone walks around inside the designated play area.

HOP—Hop inside the play area.

JUMP—Jump straight up and down once.

TWIZZLE—Jump up and turn 360 degrees before landing.

FREEZE 1,2,3,4,5,6,7,8,9,10! — Children must be completely frozen by the time the leader gets to 10. I usually do the counting as fast as I can to add a bit of pressure, excitement and silliness.

You will quadruple the fun factor if you use the FREEZE command often. If you catch someone moving after giving the FREEZE command, point it out in a fun way.

Highlight the children who are as still as statues or make goofy faces to try to unfreeze them. Then move right back into the commands and get everyone moving again. There are no points for the most frozen children and no penalties for the unfrozen. Once your group is familiar with the game, look for a volunteer to give the commands.

Variations

Add more commands each time you play— Crab Walk, Crawl, Walk Backwards, Walk on all Fours.

Twizzle with a BEAT

Each time you give a command for a movement beat a drum, or a box, or a mixing bowl. The children move to the rhythm of the beat.

Speed Rabbit Twizzle

Include animals in your commands as you would in *Speed Rabbit*—Rabbit! Freeze 1,2,3,4,5,6,7,8,9,10, Elephant! Freeze 1,2,3,… Giraffe! Freeze 1,2,3,…

People to People Twizzle

Add *People to People* commands to your list.

Peanut Butter and Jelly Stretch

Michelle Stuckey, a dance teacher in Portland, ME has shared so many movement ideas with me. Movement activities lend themselves well to adventure play. Here is one of her wonderful ways to stretch.

Space   Small

Props   None

How to Play

> The children sit on the floor with their legs stretched out in front of them. Tell your group they are going to stretch out many of the muscles in their bodies while making a peanut butter and jelly sandwich and then eating it. Rubbing their hands up and down their legs, the children first spread the peanut butter. Do this 3 or 4 times. Next, have the children reach their arms straight up to the sky, then reach down to their hips and spread more peanut butter back up their torso (better tell them what a torso is!) until they again reach back up to the sky. Repeat this stretch 3 or 4 times.
>
> Now cut the sandwich in half—legs go out to the sides. Finally, we get to eat the sandwich! Tell the children to bring their heads down to their left knee, nibble, nibble… Right knee, nibble, nibble.

Painting Rainbows

From this final position of the *Peanut Butter and Jelly Stretch*, legs in a split position, or as close as bodies allow, stretch your hands and reach out to your left toes, then sweep your arms up and over to your right toes in an arc. Go back and forth each time adding a new color, "Paint the red into the rainbow. Now paint the rainbow purple," etc.

Back to the Earth and Cobra

The ideal way to do *Back to the Earth* is on a gorgeous grassy field. The earth smells delicious. But even if you don't have access to green grass, give this one a try. It sets a peaceful mood.

Space   Small

Props   None

Back to the Earth

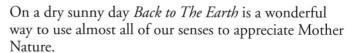

How to Play

On a dry sunny day *Back to The Earth* is a wonderful way to use almost all of our senses to appreciate Mother Nature.

Start by getting down on hands and knees and feel the grass, the earth, taking note of all the details—how does it smell, feel, sound? Ask the children what they notice.

Then move down to your bellies and put your hands under your chin. Smell the earth, look around, listen. Again ask the children for the details they notice.

Finally remove your hands and put your nose right into the grass or rest your cheeks on the grass. Ahh... Move into the *Cobra Stretch* from here

Cobra

How to Play

While still lying on the ground, put your hands back
under your chin, elbows pointing straight out like
butterflies wings. Lift your head off your chin. Next lift
your feet up and bend the knees so that your feet point
to your head. Lastly, grab your feet and arch your back,
rocking back and forth.

Bean Bag Games

There are dozens of games to play with these fun little toys. They are very easy to make, no patterns necessary and fabric remnants are inexpensive. I have had children personalize their own bean bags by coloring them with fabric markers. I sew the pieces together and the children fill them with beans at the next session. We play with the bean bags throughout the program, and children keep their personalized bean bags. (Refer back to Chapter Three for more instructions on making bean bags.)

Space   Small to large

Props   Bean Bags

Bean Bag Obstacle Course

How to Play

Children balance a bean bag on their head as they move along a designated trail. The Cumberland Head Start teachers that I have worked with set up a trail of construction paper feet around their room that shows the children which way to travel. Make the obstacle course challenging but doable for your children—around chairs, under tables, over toys, etc.

Bean Bag Tag

How to Play

Any variation of tag works well, just add an element of challenge. "You can only be walking when your bean bag is on your head." This slows down the pace of *Pairs Tag* quite well.

Bean Bag Bocci

How to Play

Set up a small hoop inside a larger circle. All children stand outside the larger circle and try to toss their bean bag into the center circle.

Obstacle Course

Obstacle courses can transform a familiar play space into an adventurous new world that can be traveled in dozens of ways.

Space   Medium

Props   Whatever you have… ropes, spots, carpet squares, construction paper foot prints, mats, tables

How to Play

Arrange a trail of poly spots, ropes or footprints around the playground or classroom. Go through tight spaces and under tables, over chairs or benches. The more changes in terrain, the more exciting the obstacle course.

Vary the method of travel to create different experiences. For example: walk backwards, crab walk, hop on one foot, pairs walk together, etc.

Variations

Add vertical hanging objects such as toys hanging from ropes that the children must avoid touching as they move along the trail.

Sticky Buddies on the Obstacle Course

Tape two children together to move along the obstacle course. Use larger stepping areas such as carpets or two poly spots side by side so that they can successfully move side by side.

Scooter Course

If you have scooters or trikes available, create a roadway for children to travel along. They can do this individually or in pairs. One person rides on the scooter and the other pulls them along with a rope or bandanna. Or have children pretend they are vehicles—pick your own—and pretend to follow the road. Create a series of traffic laws to follow and issue *tickets* for violators.

Safety Note +

Situate yourself as a spotter any time you involve climbing or balancing in your obstacle course.

Child Sort

Category games are popular in the adventure world. This one is a nice way to form small groups arbitrarily for other activities or just for the sake of identifying similarities with others.

Space   Small

Props   None

Set Up

Call out categories and ask children who fit the category to come into the middle of the circle. Acknowledge the children by confirming that they fit the category, "Billy is wearing red."

Category ideas:

Blue eyes

Green Eyes

Brown eyes

Wearing green

Wearing sneakers

Anyone with an M in their name

Left handed

Has a pet

Has a little brother or sister

Has a big brother or sister

Chapter 6

Buddy Games

Buddy Games are activities that help young children begin developing their cooperative skills and can be used as lead-ins to larger group activities. For preschoolers and elementary students (and for many older students as well), two children can be a large group. Working in twosomes can present a number of challenges to young children...

• to agree to work with a buddy

• to be aware of your buddy as you play the game

• to take care of your buddy

• to communicate with your buddy (talking with and listening to them)

• to accomplish a task together

The Partnering Progression

The first level of cooperation is an ability to work well with one other person. The next level of cooperation is to work well with new buddies, that is buddies other than a child's closest and very best friends. I call this the *partnering progression*. Children move along this progression as they develop a sense of comfort and confidence in themselves and as they develop a sense of trust in the group. Acquiring the skills and motivation to work with a variety of buddies will enhance their ability to work cooperatively within a larger group.

Be prepared for the simple act of partnering-up to be a major challenge for your group. Allowing children to choose their own partners often means someone gets left without one. Adding this lone player to a pair to make a triad can require discussion and negotiation. The alternative to this free-form partnering is to structure the process—counting off, lining up and folding the line in half, etc. Unfortunately, these methods have their own drawbacks, not the least of which is a pair refusing to work with each other.

Children are very honest about who they feel comfortable and uncomfortable with. When children refuse to pair up with one another, teachers need to respond with sensitivity. These are the occasions when the Full Value Contract becomes real. Respect each child's feelings and honor their discomfort about pairing up with the other child. Difficulties with partnering are as much related to a child's sense of safety as they are related to group dynamics. To force two children to pair up will only diminish their trust in you. Chances are their involvement in the activity will be limited, since their focus will remain on the partner assigned to them. Be quick at finding another partner or a twosome that can handle a third. Don't spend a lot of time working out the situation. Find a comfortable place for everyone and move on.

Use the games as teaching opportunities. Give your group time to talk about meeting new friends. Talk about respect, kindness and working together. Point out these behaviors as you notice them, and you will surely see the children growing and developing.

Puzzle Pairs

This activity can be used early on in your program to assist with the partnering process—helping the children become comfortable partnering up with someone who isn't their "best buddy in the whole world." Play several rounds to give the children many brief buddy experiences.

Space   Small

Props   Use square pieces of foam core, construction paper or cardboard to create two-piece puzzles.

How to Play

After distributing one puzzle part to each child ask them to try to find the person who has the mate to their puzzle piece. Once they have found their partner, collect the pieces and redistribute them. On your next round, give the partners a task to perform once they find each other. Try: tossing a fleece ball back and forth, shaking hands—

...doing a leap frog over each other twice

...doing a Row, Row, Row your Boat or *Maple Syrup Pull Up*

...solving a math problem

...telling your buddy your favorite kind of ice cream

Variation

Jigsaw Hunt

Create three or four piece puzzles using cardboard or magazine pictures cut into puzzle pieces. Children each take one piece and search for their partners.

For an easier challenge, make the puzzle squares of different colors to provide more cues for finding partners.

Once the puzzle pairs find each other and the children seem comfortable with their partners, move right into another game, such as *People to People* or *Sticky Buddies*. This will help you avoid selecting pairs for these new activities.

Sticky Buddies

This is an excellent trust-building activity and easy to vary according to the skills of your group. It came to me as I watched a three-legged race at a Fourth of July picnic. The winners of the race ran faster than most people could alone. The level of trust and cooperation between the two runners had to have been huge. I wondered how I could bring that experience to young children. Here is the idea that came to me.

Space   Large

Props   Masking tape

How to Play

Tape pairs of children together at the waist. 1 1/2 wraps secures the connection but still allows the tape to break if the children are not working well together.

Their task is to work together so that their tape connection doesn't break. *Before going anywhere*, have each pair perform some basic movements: turn around in a circle, bend and touch your toes together, take a step forward, backward, etc.

Once you have warmed them up, lead the children around the playground or gym. A course that goes around, over, under various obstacles is more fun and will challenge their skills to cooperate.

When a pair splits apart, give the pairs an opportunity to exercise their problem-solving skills… "Why did your tape break?" "What is the message the broken tape is giving you?" "What can you do to make sure it doesn't break again?"

Variations

Bandanna Buddies

Some children do not want to be taped together. Have them hold hands or hold opposite ends of a bandanna.

Give the children choices on where they want to be taped together—arms, wrists, legs, ankles…

Cooperative walking

Without being taped together, have pairs walk in unison, left legs then right legs. Triple up and do the same, then keep adding group members until ultimately everyone is doing the *Cooperative Walk*.

Tape three, four and five people together and follow a leader around the course.

Safety Note   +

Be ready to spot pairs that are not stable or don't quite understand how to take care of each other.

Maple Syrup Pull Up

This is the old favorite cooperative activity *Stand Up* with a new name. It is a wonderful team activity and you can do it anywhere because it involves no props and can be done in the smallest of spaces.

Space   Cozy

Props   None

How to Play

In pairs have the children sit on the floor facing each other. Their toes should be touching so they will need to bend their knees and skooch in close together.

If you want to be imaginative tell them that the maple syrup factory has sprung a leak in their storage tower and the sticky goo has surrounded us. We need to try to stand up without putting our hands on the ground, only by touching toes and holding our partner's hands.

The ultimate challenge for each pair to pull themselves up to a standing position. By holding hands and simultaneously pulling—remind the children to be gentle—the pairs should be able to pull themselves up.

Variations

Double and Large Group Pull Ups

Once successful at the *Pull Up* in pairs, keep adding 2 people and eventually try to do the pull up with the whole group.

Row, Row, Row Your Boat

If the *Pull Up* is too challenging, have partners get into the same feet together position. Holding hands they pull each other back and forth singing, "Row, Row, Row Your Boat."

People to People

This is a classic cooperative game. It's a fun activity for children—helping them to think about names for body parts while unselfconsciously buddying up with a number of different people.

Space   Small

Props   None

How to Play

Have the children find a partner or create pairs yourself. Or better yet, start this one with *Puzzle Pairs*.

Tell the children they need to follow your directions and connect part of their body to part of their buddy's body. For example, say, "Foot to Foot." The pairs should put one foot to their partner's foot.

Keep the body parts the same initially before moving on to more complex commands such as "Elbow to Shoulder." After five or six commands, yell "PEOPLE TO PEOPLE!" This means everyone finds a new partner.

What will follow is a moment of chaotic running around while the children find someone new. If your group is not comfortable with changing partners without much conflict, just skip this part. Stick with the same partner for as long as the group is excited about playing. Four- and five-year-olds are often ready for a new game before they are ready to change partners.

If one of the children is interested in calling out the commands let them do so while you take a partner. (You may need to help with the commands.)

Command Variations

Choose commands that are fitting for the age group you are playing with:

...touch your partner's belly

...touch your partner's head

...finger to shoulder

...back to back

...head to hand

...knee to knee

...toe to toe

...knee to shoulder

...elbow to elbow

...elbow to thumb

...toe to knee

...shoulder to pinkie

Sticky Heads

Instead of head to head, call out, "Sticky Heads" or "Sticky Toes." This means to stick head or toes or whatever together.

Drum Beats

In between commands beat a drum or clap your hands to a rhythm. Have the children move to the rhythm of the beat.

Double and Triple People to People

While maintaining the first connection, the pairs must complete the second and even third commands.

Beach Ball Balance and Beach Ball Trolley

This is a fun way to transition from one place to another—and a whole lot more exciting than lining up and walking quietly!

Space Medium and large

Props Beach balls, any soft balls, toys

How to Play

Have partners balance a ball between their heads, bellies, backs, arms and then move to your new destination or around a designated course.

Try different objects to vary the challenge.

Children with a good working partnerships may want greater challenges, such as: crawling, fast walking or balancing the object between the back of their heads, between shoulders, backs, etc.

Variation

Beach Ball Trolley

Have three, four or five children line up facing the same direction. You'll need one less ball than the number of children in each group. The challenge is for the group to walk together balancing the balls about belly-high in the spaces between them. Sound easy? Try it! (This activity is also included in the Circle Games Section with a little more detail.)

Sam Goodman, Age 7

Milk Jug Games

These scooping, catching and pouring games are especially fun if you have lots and lots of balls and big buckets or laundry baskets to be filled. I buy the balls designed for ball pits. They come in great basic colors, 100 per box. I can guarantee that the children will want to climb in with the balls before any activity begins—great play all by itself!

Space   Medium

Props   Gallon-size plastic milk jugs—one per player scissors for adults to create the scoop, lots of balls

How to Play

Cut the bottom of plastic milk jugs horizontally all the way around so that you leave a fair-sized catching scoop as you hold the handle.

If you have the time and ambition, spray paint (markers and tempera paint don't stick to the plastic) the milk jugs different colors to make them more snazzy looking. The colors can be used for grouping children or adding to their learning.

Scooping and Pouring

Four-year-olds love to scoop balls off the ground or out of a big bin and transfer them into other containers. The game is as simple as that! No relay racing, no timing, no teams…

Scooping and Pouring Relay

Older children will be looking for more complex tasks. Try incentives such as getting all the yellow balls into one container, blue into another, etc. The team with the yellow scoops gets the yellow balls…

Pairs Catching and Pairs Pouring

Toss a soft ball or bean bag to each other trying to catch it with the scoop.

Younger children may not be able to catch the ball. Let them pour one or several balls back and forth. Their fun will be in the chasing dropped balls as well as the thrill of watching many balls being poured into their jug.

Group Catch

Toss as many balls as you can into the air at once. See how many balls can be caught for a team total. This one is great fun and children tend to care less about the score than the thrill of the action.

Rolling Toes to Toesies

On a dry, warm day there is nothing more playful than rolling on the grass. And if there is even the slightest hill, what else is one inspired to do but roll down! When was the last time you rolled down a hill? Don't just watch, join in! *Do* play this game, even if you are indoors.

Space   Large

Props   None

How to Play

Lay flat on the floor or ground and stretch your arms way out. Then roll slowly—one rotation at a time. This will give the children a good picture of rolling (and of you having fun). Don't assume, as I once did, that all children know how to roll.

Now give the children an opportunity to roll on their own.

After rolling solo for a few minutes, challenge the children to try rolling with a buddy—keeping their feet and toes touching while they roll. They will need to roll slowly, keeping an eye out and feeling with their feet for their partners.

Tractor Roll

This is a group roll, in unison, in the same direction. Have the children lie down, shoulder to shoulder, and all together roll one turn at a time toward a goal (10 yards or so away). Children can not roll onto or over one another and therefore must communicate clear messages to each other… "catch up to me Jack! …go slower Ellie!… wait for me Dottie!"

Feathers and Scarves

Michelle Stuckey, my dance teacher friend from Portland, Maine uses milkweed pod seeds to inspire her dancers with ways to move their bodies. Upon seeing her lead this activity, I thought about all the balloon games we play with older participants but for safety reasons cannot play with this age group. Craft feathers and scarves float softly to the ground, making it fun and easy for young hands to catch. There is nothing more fun than chasing a floating scarf on a windy day!

Space Small (except when catching scarves outside on a breezy day, then you'll need a large open space)

Props Feathers—craft stores sell them in bright colors of all different sizes milkweed seeds— from mother nature scarves— made of lightweight material (see chapter 4 to get ideas for creating your own)

How to Play

Give the children a feather or scarf and let them experiment with throwing or blowing it into the air and then catching it.

Don't be surprised if this keeps them happily playing for 10 minutes.

Try dropping the scarves and feathers as you stand on a chair. Invite the children to try catching the feather/scarf on their knee, shoulder, foot, back, head, etc.

Variations

Scarf Variation

In pairs, the children scrunch up their scarves, and on the count of three, toss their scarves to their partners.

Toss and Twirl

Toss the scarf into the air, spin around once and try to catch the scarf before it hits the ground.

Feathers and Fans

Break out the largest fan you have. Toss feathers into the air currents created by the fan. Try to catch the feathers as above, with knees, arms, heads, etc. Good outdoor kind of fun on a long, indoor winter kind of day!

Scarf Jumping

Have the children lay their scarves on the floor, flattening them out. Jump over, hop over with two feet together, hop over each corner with one foot, crab walk over, etc.

Caveat

On a very windy day, your scarves will fly beyond your playground walls and into the nearest tree. So wait for a gentle breeze to play this one.

Safety Notes   +

When children are chasing scarves, they involve themselves in the pursuit so totally that it is not uncommon for them to not know where they are going. Spot carefully so that no one runs into a tree or a classmate!

For safety reasons balloons are often banned from schools because they are a choking hazard if not blown up and in the little pieces they break into when popped. Balloon games have been intentionally excluded from this book for this reason and should probably be avoided in games sessions with this age group. Scarves, feathers and beach balls are great substitutes for most activities usually requiring balloons.

Chapter 7

Running, Jumping,
Fast Moving Games

Children love and need to run. They often appear their happiest and most vibrant when allowed to stretch and work legs and lungs and hearts.I have played *Beep, Times Up* with many groups of children and without exception they are not ready to move on to another activity when I am.

Consider any wide open, flat grassy space a luxury—a Bag of Tricks unto itself! You may not have access to

grassy fields on a daily basis but chances you have something reasonably close by. You might want to plan a genuine field trip to a great big field just for a session of active running games. However and whenever you find yourself in one of these open spaces, let yourself and your children soak up the wonderfulness of running freely.

Tom Zierk, editor of this book, has adapted a number of adventure games for young children and has an opening activity that asks children to run and scream as far as they can and as loud as they can in one breath. They usually give him puzzled looks when told to yell their loudest and run their fastest. It seems such a rare occur- rence for children to be told to be loud, and to run with abandon.

In your wide-open spaces you can play so many games, more than those described in this chapter of course. Try also using open spaces for Warm Ups and Body Stretches, using variations to suit your setting—skip the length of the field, throw your fleece ball as far as you can, run to it and continue throwing it until you get to the end of the field.

If you live in a region that experiences real winters, this might be the chapter to focus on when you need outdoor time. With proper outdoor clothing and nice soft snow, you and your children will be quite warm playing these highly active games. Then come inside and drink hot cocoa! It is also our job, as teachers, to create cozy cocoa memories with our children.

Beep! Time's Up

This is a great game for a group that has plenty of energy to burn. Older children, teens and adults often need slower paced games to warm them up. This is one of my favorite games for getting the wiggles out, especially since it always becomes one of the children's favorites, too.

Space   Large, room to run

Props   None

How to Play

Pick a location on the playground or gym and tell the children they only have a certain amount of time, 10 seconds for example, to get there. (Try to time it so that all children can arrive at the destination before you say beep.)

When you reach the end of your count, yell "BEEP—TIME'S UP!" Count loudly as they run—speeding up or slowing down the count as needed.

Encourage the children's ability to support and praise each other by cheering and giving high fives. If you run with them you can model this. Each run then becomes a team win and cause for celebration.

Variations

Be creative with the means of travel. Try hopping on one foot, hopping on two feet, sideways running, walking backwards, crab walking, silly walking, etc.

Add more distance to the runs and negotiate with the group how many seconds they think they'll need to get there.

Add additional instructions, such as, "Run to the soccer goal and then all sit down." or "Hop on one foot to the sand box then touch something red." "Run to the swings and then touch the tree."

Have the children partner up and hold hands as they hop or skip to the destination.

Safety Note +

Check the running area for holes or other obstacles.

Try to use a wide enough area so that the children can run with abandon and not have to compete for limited space. Too small an area can result in trips and shoving.

Beware of the competitive spirit. Some children are inclined to want to be the first and to "win" at all costs. This is a good opportunity to discuss the Be Gentle, Be Kind, Be Safe guidelines. Try shifting the focus by working in pairs.

Over the River

This game is quite reliable for capturing the enthusiasm of a group. Success and fun are always high, and it's a good activity to set the stage for more challenging group work.

Space Large

Props 2 ropes approximately 20' long

How to Play

Create a river with two ropes laid onto the ground parallel to each other. Keep them fairly close together to start—six to eight inches will do.

Line up everyone on one side of the river.

Tell your group that you are going to call out, "1, 2, 3—Over the river!" At this point, they all jump over the *river* together. As the children get better and more comfort-able with their jumping skills, widen the river little by little.

This is a good time to do some problem solving. Ask them how they can get across the river when it is about three, four or five feet wide. (Hint… You will most likely have a range of jumping abilities in your group so squiggle the far side of the river.) Let the children choose where they want to stand.

This age group loves an added drama of *the shark*. I tell them if they don't get across the river, the sharks will nip at their feet. Some children prefer falling into the river, rolling and kicking their feet into the air and screaming "shark!" even more than the jumping over the river.

Variations

Invite the group to try jumping over the river while holding hands.

Build a series of rivers in a row. Once the group crosses one river, the next river, a wider one, is already waiting for them. If you've got plastic sharks throw them in the river for effect.

Safety Note   +

The greatest injury potential in this game is head to head bumps when children are traveling in opposite directions. To avoid this, always have children jump over the river in one direction only. Once a jump is complete, play traffic officer by holding up your hand—STOP! This also gives you a chance to widen the river for another round.

Musical Pairs

Unfortunately, the original Musical Chairs is alive and well today—the one that eliminates both chairs and children. We can do our best to eliminate that exclusionary version with this alternative. Adding music to your games will awaken a whole new dynamic in the group. Doing the *Trust Circle* is a helpful prerequisite for *Musical Pairs*.

Space   Large

Props   Tape player and fast, fun music

How to Play

Pair up the kids and have them stand with elbows interlocked.

When you turn on the music children walk away from their partners. It's best to use the bumpers up—hands at face level, palms out—position here. Remind children to be gentle with each other as they move about.

Once the music stops partners need to quickly get back together, locking elbows once again.

Start the music again and they drift apart.

Stop the music and they find each other.

Try starting and stopping the music very quickly for extra giggles.

Give the children instructions on how to move to the music—fly like birds, crawl, jump, etc.

Variations

Give each pair a home base, such as a carpet square or hoop. The pairs of children begin inside their home base, move away when the music plays, and return when it stops.

Safety Note +

Teach the children "bumpers up" walking. Bend your arms at the elbows and hold your hands in front of your face, palms out, about a foot in front. This will prevent bumps of heads and noses that can happen when children are moving quickly all at the same time.

Pairs Tag

This is a simple game of I chase you, then you chase me. Players change roles from *It* to *Chasee* so often that the fun factor stays high longer than their energy holds up.

Space　Large

Props　Boundary markers

How to Play

Establish boundaries with rope, markers or natural boundaries. The boundary should be large enough so the group can move around comfortably.

Create pairs of children and then have one child from each pair decide to be *It* first.

All the children will be playing tag with their partner at the same time. Because this can get a little crazy, this is a WALKING ONLY tag game. (I have played *Pairs Tag* successfully with seven- and eight-year-olds, but it can be difficult for preschoolers to contain themselves to this walking only restriction.) Some children have a difficult time understanding this rule… a tag game without running? They can't imagine that it will be fun—until they play a round.

The children who are It chase their partners. Once an It catches their partner, they reverse roles.

Before chasing the new Chasee, the new It needs to spin around once.

Play a demonstration round with a partner to give children a visual understanding of how to play.

The game continues until you declare "Time Out!"

Play several rounds changing partners and/or shrinking or enlarging the boundaries.

Variations

When groups have demonstrated an ability to take care of one another (Be Gentle), try playing several rounds gradually shrinking the boundaries so it becomes very cozy.

Require players to sing a line from a song while they spin around before going after their partner—Old MacDonald or Twinkle Twinkle Little Star or a song they just learned in class.

Pairs Pairs Tag

Play in foursomes with two teams of two. The It team interlocks elbows, the Chasee team does the same. The challenge is to stay together while on the chase or being chased. A tag only counts if the It team is intact.

Safety Note +

Teach players the Bumpers Up position— elbows bent, hands in front of your face, palms out. You will need to reinforce both Bumpers Up and walking only throughout the game. To avoid head and nose bumps, ducking down or squatting down are not allowed.

Larry the Lizard

Kristen Cameron, an occupational therapist in Maine, has introduced Larry the Lizard to her group. He comes along whenever she is doing group games. Anyone who chooses to not participate in an activity is given the responsibility of holding Larry. This gives shy and reluctant children a role in the activity and allows them to participate in a way that feels comfortable and safe. When these children are ready to participate to a greater degree, they can still hold Larry or help him participate in the activity.

Use any stuffed animal or object that appeals to or has special meaning for you and your group.

Run, Rabbit, Run

This is a classic physical education and playground game similar to Octopus… a must have for your games repertoire.

Space   Large

Props   Cones, ropes or tape to mark boundary lines

How to Play

> Set up two parallel lines 30 to 60 feet apart. If your playing area is quite large, set up side boundaries as well.
>
> Have the group stand behind one line.
>
> Ask two volunteers to be foxes.
>
> The rest of the group are rabbits and do not want to be caught by the foxes.
>
> The foxes stand inside the boundaries.
>
> When the foxes yell "Run, Rabbit, Run!" the entire group of rabbits must run through the playing area

without being tagged by the foxes. They must stay inside the boundaries.

Once the group of rabbits reaches the other side, they are safe. Rabbits who have been tagged (or who have gone out of bounds), stay frozen where they were tagged.

The game continues when the foxes again yell, "Run, Rabbits, Run!" Each round will result in more frozen rabbits until, eventually, there are no more rabbits left to run.

Variations

The foxes can give the rabbits a command that they must perform before running across the field. For example: shake hands with one person, spin around three times.

Once tagged, rabbits become the foxes helpers. They remain frozen in one place but their hands can reach out and tag other rabbits as they run by.

Everyone, including the fox does the crab walk, or crawls on hands and knees.

The fox calls out a color. Only the children wearing that color runs across.

Peek-a-Who?

As described here, *Peek-a-Who* results in differing outcomes for younger children. I have had fun playing with preschoolers, and so have the children, but they often end up just staring at the other child and laughing. *Monkey Under The Blanket*, on the next page, works better for younger children.

Space   Small

Props   Blanket or sheet

How to Play

Ask two people (adults) to hold a sheet or blanket between them so that it hangs to the floor like a curtain.

Divide the children into two equal-size groups.

Each group picks a side of the blanket to squat down behind so that the other team cannot see them.

Send one child per team to kneel right in front of the blanket. On the count of three, drop the blanket. The object is for the children at the blanket, who are now staring directly at each other, to say the name of the child as quickly as possible. Whoever says the other's name first gets to bring that child onto their team. The objective is to have one team with everyone on it.

Variations

Have the two children at the blanket face their group (so their back's are to the blanket). Each group tries to help their partner guess the name of the other team's player by describing the child on the other side of the blanket. The descriptions should not, obviously, include the child's name! Be careful that the descriptions are positive.

Monkey Under the Blanket

This is a variation of an activity from Marianne Torbert's book, *Follow Me, A Handbook of Movement Activities*. It is a nice detective-like guessing game to play with a large group.

Space Small

Props Blanket

How to Play

Divide the group into two teams.

Send one group out of the room or to the other end of the room. Ask them to hide their eyes.

The other group chooses one member to hide under the blanket. The group hiding their eyes returns and tries to guess which *Monkey* is under the blanket. To give everyone an opportunity to guess, you can have the children whisper their guesses into your ear instead of shouting them out.

Provide clues if the group needs them, like sticking a foot or hand out from under the blanket, or making noises. Children who have guessed correctly can whisper the answer into other children's ears.

End each round with a group shout. "One, two, three…!" Everyone shouts the name of the child under the blanket.

Variations

Put two children under the blanket at the same time.

Hide an object under the blanket and allow the guessing team to feel the object through the blanket. Also allow the guessing team to ask questions of the other team.

Wiggly Worm

This one is a terrific game to play when you want to draw a crowd. (My daughter Maggie actually invented it the very first time I opened my game bag for her and my son, Freddy.) Start with two or three children and before you know it you'll have 10 more who want to play and can easily join right in.

Space Medium

Props Ropes, 10 to 20 feet long

How to Play

Tie one end of your rope to a fence post or leg of a table right at ground level.

Wiggle the rope to create *waves,* making sure that the rope stays on the ground. (If raised even an inch or two, the rope will cause tripping.)

The object is to jump over the *Wiggly Worm* without touching it. Keep traffic going in one direction for safety reasons. When you need a little more excitement, add one or two more worms.

If a child wants to be a wiggler be ready to help make sure that the rope stays on the ground.

Variation

I have found that some children prefer to step on the *worms.* If this is the inclination of your group, go for it. Just wiggle the ropes a little faster!

Safety Note +

Keep those ropes right down on the ground or the game will rapidly become a trust breaker!

Chapter 8

Trust Building and Group Problem Solving Activities

All children fall somewhere along a continuum of being cautious to being trusting. Some children unconsciously and eagerly put themselves in the trust of others. Others are more reticent in giving their trust. Learning how and when to trust others—both emotionally and physically—is important for children. Adventure games and activities are an engaging way for children to begin learning skills that they will use throughout their entire lives.

Trust Building and Group Problem Solving Activities have long been essential components of adventure programs. Adventure activities offer a unique and effective way to help people work together and to appreciate the diverse skills and talents individuals bring to any group process. Even very young children will begin to trust, appreciate and understand the role of their classmates in solving problems as a group.

As teachers, we can play an active role in moving children—both as individuals and in groups—along the continuum toward cooperation and trust. Working to make the learning environment safe for all the children in your group is an ongoing process. Each time they play together in cooperative ways and are presented with games and activities that challenge their ability to work together they will further their sense of trust in other individuals and in the group. Constant attention to how children treat each other along with consistent reminders to be gentle, kind and safe will steadily move children toward more cooperative and trusting dealings with each other.

Trust Circle

This is my favorite activity to use as a beginning group trust builder and problem solver. It is adaptable to all ages, stages of group development and group sizes.

Space   Medium

Props   Rope, poly spots or tape

How to Play

Create a large circle with a rope, poly spots or tape. All participants take a place around the circle facing the middle.

Demonstrate the bumpers up position (arms outstretched, elbows slightly bent, palms facing out at about face height) and have everyone put their bumpers up. On a command of "Go," the challenge is for everyone in the group to cross the circle without touching anyone else.

All the children should end up on the opposite side of the circle, or close to it, from where they began but need not take a straight course to get there.

Check in and see how many touches the group had. Don't assign consequences for touches, just set a goal for reducing the number and try again.

Variations

To add a degree of difficulty, time how long it takes for everyone to get across to their new place—still without touching anyone.

Triangle, Square, Circle

This is an easier version that may be more successful with larger groups. Give each child a piece of paper with a triangle, square or circle drawn on it. Call out one shape at a time and only those children holding that shape move across the circle. After a round or two have everyone trade cards. If you don't have your shape props ready to go, assign each child one of three animals. Or distribute equal numbers of balls, poly spots or bandannas from your game bag. "All the people with bandannas change places."

Up and Down the River

This is a *Trust Circle* version I have played with four- and five-year-olds. Create a river, long and wide with your rope. Have everyone step inside the river and imagine they are fish, turtles, frogs, etc. When you say go the children pretend they are one of these animals and move up and down the river, again without touching anyone else. Younger children are quite expressive about the roles they take on and have a lot of fun with the activity because of this dramatic twist. They may even "dry off" at the end of the game!

Car and Driver, aka Trust Walk

This activity can build a child's trust in you or another child. I tend toward not using blindfolds so that Challenge By Choice can be defined by each child. I call it *Peeking By Choice*.

Space   Large

Props   None

How to Play

> Break your group into pairs.
>
> One child in each pair keeps their eyes open and plays the role of the DRIVER. The other child in the pair close their eyes—they are the CARS. Drivers stand behind their Cars, guiding them around a course.
>
> Establish the course the driver and car follow. A wide-open field is a good place to play this. I like to do this activity initially one pair at a time, coaching the Cars on how to communicate with their partners. As you begin to trust the group you can have more than one pair go at a time.
>
> Never assume, however, that a group has the knowledge or maturity to do this safely from the start. Children will generally peek a lot but there are children who really go for the full eyes closed experience and you need to be ready to help out if their driver is not providing them with a safe ride.

Don't be too concerned if the Car's eyes are open the entire time. The children are *growing their way* and are likely still having fun.

Variations

A Walk Through The Forest

Children scatter about the play space with arms stretched up and out as though they are trees. One pair at a time walks or "drives" through the forest, avoiding the trees and branches.

Sherpa Walk

If your group has successfully completed the *Trust Walk*, they may be ready for this more challenging group walk.

Space   Large open

Props   None

How to Play

Ask for two volunteers. These two children are the Sherpas or Guides who lead the group of mountaineers up a treacherous mountain side (you create the route). The fog is dense and only the sherpas know the route will enough to navigate through it.

The mountaineers must hold hands, close their eyes and stay in a line, one behind the other—not side by side. This is hard to do for many children but it is important for their safety.

Don't let a line be longer than four children—the ones in the back tend to forge their own trail rather than following the path of the leader.

The original version of this game for adults and older youths has the sherpas communicating nonverbally with the mountaineers—clapping hands, grunting, etc. Sherpas are also not allowed to touch the mountaineers. This is definitely too challenging for four- to eight-year-olds! Have one Sherpa hold hands with the front person and the other Sherpa hold hands with the last person. This way they can gently guide the group physically and verbally throughout the walk.

Variation

Try letting every other child keep their eyes open.

Pairs of children, one with eyes open, one with eyes closed, can walk in a line with you as the guide.

Safety Note +

Choose a path that is both challenging and safe for your group. Walk closely with the group and be prepared to stop the activity if the children are not concentrating and acting safely.

Sidebar Note

Stopping an Activity

There may be times when you need to call an end to an activity. Perhaps the level of chaos is too high, the children are not acting kindly, or you just feel the situation is unsafe. Use this as a teachable moment. Try not to be discouraged or angry with the children. Bring the group together for a short, sit-down discussion. Ask them if they know why they needed to stop. What could they do to make the game more fun, safer, less chaotic?

If you think they are up to it, try the activity again. Remember that in some cases trying again may not work. Just because they know what went wrong doesn't mean they have the skills to fix it.

The Clock

This classic Project Adventure Game is a variation of *Duck Duck Goose* and *Ring Around The Rosie*, games we all grew up with. Don't tell your children this, however. As I set up this game one child asked me skeptically, "You're not going to have us play *Duck, Duck Goose*, are you?" "Of course not," I said to his relief.

Space   Large, open

Props   4 cones or other markers

How to Play

> Get the group into a circle, your first major challenge.
>
> Put a marker at 12, 3, 6 and 9 o'clock.
>
> All players sit in a circle outside these markers holding hands, the second major challenge.
>
> Walk through the activity once as you give the group directions. On "GO" the task is for all the children to stand up, WALK clockwise around the markers, get back to their starting spots and sit back down—all without breaking hands—the third major challenge.
>
> Younger children will not know what clockwise means or what 12, 3, 6, and 9 o'clock are for that matter. The activity still works—just scrap the clock. "We'll move around the circle in this direction until we get back to our original spots."

Variations

> Four- and five-year-olds do better moving around a solid object such as a sheet or a hoop. Staying outside the markers is hard for them to conceptualize. They also love to have a song to sing as the move. Try this one...

Motor boat, motor boat, go so slow,

Motor boat, motor boat, go so slow,

Motor boat, motor boat, step on the gas

Motor boat, motor boat, go so fast

Motor boat, motor boat, go so fast

Motor boat, motor boat, out of gas

Motor boat, motor boat, chug, chug chug

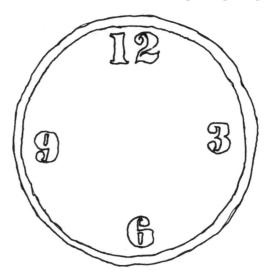

To increase the challenge have the group do *The Clock* at a fast walk. Running doesn't usually work, you'll end up with several children going to the ground.

An even more advanced challenge: when the person at 12 o'clock gets back to start have them (or you) yell "REVERSE," and go counterclockwise (that way), get back to start and then all sit down.

Safety Note   +

Make sure this activity is done walking. Be careful when/if you move the pace up to a fast walk. Smaller children can easily be overpowered by bigger and stronger children and get pulled down or tripped.

Sleepy Snakes' Snake Pit

This game adds a new dimension to trust. Try it if your group has had success with the *Trust Circle* and the *Trust Walk*.

Space   Small

Props   Several ropes

How to Play

Put the ropes into a squiggly arrangement on the floor—like many snakes intertwined.

Initially leave large open spaces around the ropes.

So as not to instill a new phobia in the minds of your youngsters, tell them they are looking at lots of friendly but sleeping snakes—our pets. When you say GO, the children will try to walk through the snakes' bedroom without stepping on any of them and without bumping into each other. Start with small numbers going through one at a time—similar to the *Trust Circle*. Gradually work your way up to the entire group going through at once.

Some children will gingerly tiptoe through, others will zip through as fast as they can. As you start to feel more comfortable with their ability to take care of one another, the real challenge in this game, you can increase the challenge. Add more ropes, tighten up the spaces between ropes, have children continue walking around the snakes bedroom instead of exiting at the opposite side.

Variations

For younger groups, have everyone go through the snake pit in the same direction. This is a safer version for children who are still more egocentric and are unable to be fully aware of others.

Sticky Buddies in The Snake Pit

Go through the sleepy snake circle in pairs taped together at the waist.

Quick Line Up

This is a game that you can play over and over. Younger groups appreciate the repetition, giving them a chance to really understand the activity. *Quick Line Up* challenges childrens' sense of direction as well as their awareness of others.

Space   Open

Props   Tape or ropes to create a square... 4 different-colored bandannas

How to Play

Create a square with ropes or tape, large enough for your whole group to stand around.

Divide the group into four equal teams. (It helps to have twelve or more children for this activity to create the square.) Try creatively breaking up a group—it becomes a fun activity in itself. For example, everyone born in January, February and March becomes one group, April, May and June another, etc. Or whoever is wearing a red T-shirt becomes a team, white, blues, etc. If one team is overwhelmingly larger than the others, recruit a few to the team that needs people.

Have each team stand on one side of the square facing into the middle.

Stand in the middle and ask the children to notice which part of your body they are facing. To give the groups additional clues, wear four different colored bandannas: one on each arm, one tucked into the front of your shirt and one tucked into your belt on your back side.

Tell the children that they always need to face the same side of you that they are looking at now.

You are going to spin around like an airplane with your arms stretched out to the sides. Once you put your arms down the children can begin to move their whole team so that they are positioned to the same side they are facing now. *They must move with bumpers up and without touching anyone.*

Walk through these directions once slowly to demonstrate. When a group is lined up in the proper orientation, they raise their hands and yell, "QUICK LINE UP!"

Give a cheer for each team as they get into position. But keep the action going, the fun is in the movement.

Once you have done a few rounds, try moving (like an airplane, remember) to a place outside the square. The group can move only after you have put your arms down.

Safety Note +

Before you begin, remind the children that they need to be gentle as they reposition themselves. Use the Bumpers Up position as they move to protect heads. It is far safer to require that groups move to their new location without touching anyone else. Children like this additional challenge and everyone seems to be happier playing this way.

Try playing *Trust Circle* as a warm up to this activity.

All Aboard

Once you've done this game as described, you'll want to try it wherever you go—can everybody climb aboard a big rock? ...a fallen log? ...a sidewalk square? ...the possibilities are endless.

Space   Small

Props   One large blanket, sheet or tarp

How to Play

Spread your sheet out on the ground and ask the group to climb aboard. This is usually a simple task.

Have everyone step off and then fold the sheet in half.

Now try to get the whole group on board, making sure that everyone is on and nobody's feet are touching the ground.

Keep reducing the size of the sheet, using your judgment as to how challenging each step should be.

As the sheet gets smaller take time to discuss strategies with the children that might help them get the whole group aboard. Frustrations and other feelings may need to be aired as well.

Variations

Magic Carpet

Four- and five-year-olds enjoy the magic carpet scenario.
You can set the stage by talking about Aladin and Jas-
mine, familiar characters to many children. At each step
of the game they enjoy pretending the carpet is flying.
"I'm patting the moon!" one girl exclaimed as we rode
the magic carpet.

Top of the Mountain

Try a scenario in which the entire group is climbing Mt.
Washington or some local hill. With a little hard work
and problem solving, the peak always has room for the
whole group.

Chaotic Team Juggle

This game comes from Dr. Marianne Torbert, who has written several books on movement play for young people. Her books are a must for your library. Making the trash balls is a great way to show children that they can create their own play materials and therefore create their own fun. (See Chapter 4 for more game and prop ideas.)

Space Medium

Props Trash balls or fleece balls, about one for every three children

How to Play

Tell the children that as a group they are going to try to juggle as many balls as possible.

They can only throw a ball to a person if that person is looking directly into their eyes. Eye contact says that "I am ready for you to throw the ball to me." Play with one ball at first. When you think the children are ready, add another, and another, until many balls are in play.

If a ball falls to the ground it can simply be picked up and put back into play. Be sure to remind children to only toss the ball to a child who is looking directly at them.

Chaos is inevitable, but if there is *too* much chaos call for a freeze. You may want to reduce the number of balls if it gets too wild.

If balls continually fall to the ground you can back up and do some throwing and catching skill development in pairs or threes. Then begin the *Chaotic Group Juggle* again. When the group enjoys the chaos and is playing Gently and Safely, start adding more balls.

Variations

Silent Chaotic Team Juggle

Play *Chaotic Team Juggle* in complete silence. Children need to get each others attention nonverbally before tossing their ball.

Group Juggle

Try this one with your older children after playing *Chaotic Team Juggle* or after a tossing and catching skill development activity.

Space   Small

Props   Trash balls or fleece balls

How to Play

The first task in *Group Juggle* is to stand in a circle (start with six to eight children for the first attempt). Have a child toss the ball to another child across the circle who tosses it on to

another. Try not to let them pass the ball to a person directly beside them. After each child receives the ball have them raise their hand so that they don't get it a second time.

Ask each child to remember who they pass the ball to and who they receive it from. The last child to receive the ball tosses it to the child who began the tossing sequence.

Once the pattern is established, have the children try to repeat it—the first challenge. When you think the group remembers the pattern, start a second ball. The challenge is to "juggle" (gently toss) the balls, following the same sequence, without dropping a ball. Increase the challenge according to the readiness of your group—add more balls, or objects of different sizes (keep them soft), or increase the speed of passing.

Variations

Group Juggle Machine

Each player adopts a sound—beep, whoop, whee, yeow, pop—that they make every time they pass a ball. The effect is that of a machine doing its job.

Fun to do, funny to listen to.

Catch Up

Throwing, catching and eye contact are skills children will use in *Catch Up*. Adding a little speed and pressure increases the fun.

Space   Small

Props   3 or 4 balls or hoops

How to Play

Have the children form a circle and ask three or four volunteers to stand in the middle, facing out.

Each of these children holds a trash ball or fleece ball. Use larger balls for an easier challenge, smaller ones as players become more proficient passers and catchers.

The inner players start off with a designated outer circle player to throw to. Make sure the outer circle players are divided equally amongst the inner players. In other words, if you have 12 people on the outer circle, every fourth player will be assigned to be the first to catch the ball from an inner player. Each inner player begins by tossing their ball to an outer player who will then tosses it directly back to the inner player. That inner player will then toss it to the next person, clockwise. That outer person tosses it back to the inner player and so on.

The inner players continue to move clockwise around the circle with the ultimate goal of catching up to the other inner players who are doing exactly the same thing. If a ball is dropped, it is put back into play wherever the player left off. The round ends when an inner player's ball catches up to another player's ball. Select new inner circle players and try another round.

Hoop Islands

Musical chairs is an old classic that always ended up eliminating everyone and can become quite aggressive toward the end. This one is about music, fun and inclusion.

Space Small to large

Props Hoops, spots, homemade construction paper circles or paper plates

How to Play

Place the hoops around the room.

As the music plays the children walk anywhere but inside the hoops. When the music stops they must scramble to get inside the hoops.

Each time you play the music take one more hoop away.

Estimate the smallest number of hoops the group can fit into. Keep those hoops close together. Encourage the children to kindly and gently make room for everyone. Give a big cheer for working so well together.

Variations

If you use small spots, instruct them in the beginning that when the music stops, they need to put the toes of one foot into a spot. The other foot can be on the ground outside the spot.

Star Wars

I played *Hoop Islands* with a group of mostly seven- and eight-year-olds and called it *Star Wars*. The hoops were their space stations. I did not have access to a portable stereo so I called out the instructions to skip, walk, twirl, backwards walk, etc. I yelled *Star Wars!* when it was time for them to scramble to a hoop. I gradually eliminated space stations as above. The game was a hit, with a great deal of credit going to its very cool name!

Marshmallow River

Marshmallow River is a challenging activity for a group learning to work together. Try it two or three times with discussion and problem solving discussions between rounds. The first attempt always seems to be extra chaotic, then gradually children begin to understand ways to work together and achieve better results.

Space   Large, open

Props   Poly spots, foam squares or carpet squares

How to Play

Set up an imaginary river, marking the sides of the river with rope or masking tape 20 to 30 feet apart. Place spots, carpet squares or foam squares as a path across the river.

Be creative in setting the scene. "See that area over there (pointing to the *river* you set up)? Imagine that is a big mug full of hot chocolate. Floating on the top are giant marshmallows. We are little ants trying to cross the river by stepping on the marshmallows floating in the cocoa. We'll need to hold hands as we cross so no one falls in. Our goal is to get everyone across the cup without anyone falling in."

Help get them started by asking the group to stand in a circle. "Let's talk about how we are going to do this. How fast should we walk? Will it be hard to hold hands?"

After a bit of brainstorming and discussion, with the group in a line and holding hands attempt your first crossing.

You may find this a bit chaotic and frustrating at first (especially for the children at the end of the line). Once you have everyone across, stand in a circle again. "How did that go? Did anyone fall in? How could we do it so no one falls in or gets left behind?" (You may need to coach them to think about walking slower and taking care of the person behind.)

Now try again. This time reverse the line so the children who went last will now go first. "How did it go this time? Were we better? Why? Do you want to try again?"

And try again, if the children want to.

What a perfect game to end with some real marshmallows!

Variation

For older children more capable of small group work, instead of setting the *marshmallows* on the ground, give one to each child. The challenge for this group is to use the marshmallows (carpet squares, etc.) to cross the cup. The children put the marshmallows down on the ground as they move across the marked area. Again, they are trying not to touch the ground.

Stepping Stones

This is a more challenging version of *Marshmallow River* that is geared for seven- and eight-year-olds. It requires some problem solving and a lot of teamwork.

Space   Large open

Props   Poly spots or paper plates or carpet squares

How to Play

If you have a large group split them, creatively, into groups of 4 to 6 children.

Give each group one poly spot per child, plus one extra.

Set up an imaginary river, using ropes or masking tape, about 30 feet wide.

Tell the children they are frogs that cannot swim. They are only able to leap from lily pad to lily pad in order to get to the other side of the river. Their challenge is to work together as a group to get to the other side of the river. In order to do so, they will need to share lily pads.

Once the entire group of frogs arrives on the opposite bank they will be magically transformed back into boys and girls. Any frogs that happen to step into the river must return to the point where they fell in.

I usually ask the group to discuss their ideas before they begin solving the problem, otherwise they usually won't.

Variations

Buddies

After going solo, pair up the children and have themshare their spots to get across together.

Obstacle Course

Set out your poly spots on a trail around a play area. Put some close together and others at a long stretch. Have the course go over things like picnic tables—emphasize spotting—and under low obstacles. Put enough spots in these low areas so children can be down on all fours and still be on spots.

Solo

Give each child two poly spots and have them travel across the river using only those spots. This activity helps children work on the skill of retrieving spots and using them to move forward.

Key Punch

I like this game because there is a way to vary it no matter what your group is studying… letters, numbers, animals, planets, the web of life… you name it.

Space   Large open

Props   Poly spots with numbers or letters, rope or masking tape

How to Play

Give each child a poly spot with a designated number, one through whatever number of children you have in your group. Have the children place their spot inside a large circle outlined by rope or masking tape. This is their homemade computer key board.

Have everyone stand behind a starting line, about 20 ft. from the circle of spots. The object is for the group to run to the circle and touch their spot, one at a time, in consecutive order, and then head back to the starting line. Only one person can be inside the circle at a time. You can track their time and the number of mistakes if you want to motivate them to improve with each attempt.

Variations

Easier variation: If your group is not ready for letters or numbers, have them choose an object from your game bag. If two children pick similar items it's problem solving time! "What can you do to make sure you know this ball is yours and not Jane's?" After placing their object inside the circle, the children come back behind the starting line. One at a time, they run to the circle, retrieve their object, then tag a child to go and get their object until all the items are retrieved.

Here's a more challenging variation:

Key Punch Retrieval

Rather than arranging the numbered poly spots inside a circle, spread them out all over your playground in slightly hidden places. On GO! the children must find their number and return to the starting line. They must cross over the line to HOME in consecutive order. This requirement encourages them to help each other find their numbers. As they begin to understand how to work together better, they might be interested in timing themselves.

Treasure Hunt

This activity is like *Hide and Seek*, only with inanimate objects doing the hiding. I use a collection of stuffed animals and plastic toys because they're fun for the children and I happen to have many dozens of them in my house.

Space   Large—playground or wooded area is ideal

Props   A distinctly different object for each child

How to Play

Have each child select a different object, have them look at it, study it, name it if they want and remember it as theirs. (For as long as they are playing this game, it really is theirs'.)

Gather all the objects in a basket or bag and head out to your playground. It helps to have your group out of sight of the hunting grounds. But if that is not an option, have the children turn their backs and close their eyes.

After you have hidden all the objects, tell the group they are explorers in search of treasure. The only treasure they can bring back home is the one they began with. They can, of course, help each other so that everyone returns home as quickly as possible.

Variations

Buddy Hunt

After a round or two of hunting solo, have the children pair up. Hide all the objects again. The buddies need to be linked together throughout the hunt and return as quickly as they can with both treasures.

Buddy Hides the Object

Buddied up, with one partner closing their eyes, children hide their buddy's object. The hider returns and accompanies their partner on the search, but does not give clues unless the seeker requests them.

Team Treasure Hunt

Give everyone a numbered poly spot. After the children know their numbers, take their spots and hide them. The group links together for the search and needs to pick up the hidden polyspots in numerical order. Start with groups of four or five before attempting a larger group hunt.

Buddy Rope Shapes and Letters

Here is another game that is quite adaptable to whatever subject matter the children are learning about.

Space   Small

Props   Short pieces of rope about two or three feet long or lengths of old hose (softer, safer and more flexible)

How to Play

Give everyone a buddy rope and let them spend time jumping rope. They will want to do this anyway so why not make it part of the activity.

Then put them into groups of three and have them create a circle with their ropes. Then try triangles, letters, numbers, etc. All ropes need to be a part of the final object. If you have room to spread out, try a large group circle or square, star or city.

Variations

Buddy Rope Words

Give teams of players 10 or more Buddy Ropes and have them try to create words or pictures with their ropes that other teams then try to decipher.

Help Me, Please

The real challenge in this game is to remain on your spot and request help. Children love to be the helpers because they can move around.

Space   Large

Props   Many fleece balls and a large crate or bucket, hoops or poly spots

How to Play

Arrange most of your group on poly spots around the bucket.

Have a few children be the Helpers. When the game begins, the Helpers have all the balls.

The object of the activity is for the children on the poly spots to toss the balls into the bucket.

They must remain stuck to their spots throughout the game. When they are empty handed they yell "Help Me!" so that the Helpers know who needs a ball.

The Helpers retrieve the balls that miss and give them back to the throwers to try again. Keep on throwing and helping until all the balls are in the bucket.

Do another round or two to give other children an opportunity to be Helpers.

Variations

Milk Jug Help Me, Please

Give everyone a milk jug scoop. Play the game as above only the throwers and helpers must toss, scoop or pour the balls using their milk jug.

Buddy Help Me, Please

When a large group of children playing *Help Me, Please* becomes too chaotic and seems not to be using their ability to positively communicate with one another, it's probably time to try *Buddy Help Me, Please*. Each pair has its own bucket and six to ten balls. Throwers stand on their spot and toss balls into the bucket. If they miss, their partner, who stands watching, frozen like a statue, can be unfrozen only with a plaintive, "Will you get that ball for me?" The retriever becomes frozen again upon fetching the ball until the next call for assistance. The pairs continue until all balls are in the bucket, then children switch places.

Trust Cocoon

Credit for this activity goes to a four-year-old named Zach. While playing *Blanket Ball* he suggested that we try putting a person on the blanket and lift them up. My first reaction was that the group probably couldn't lift a child and therefore it wouldn't be safe, but then my co-teacher and I discussed it and agreed to try it out. The *Cocoon* became the hit of the day and everyone wanted another turn. With two adults participating, this activity is quite safe.

Space   Small

Props   A large
sheet or
blanket

How to Play

Have at least two adults for this activity. The adults stand on opposite sides of the blanket. Be certain that your blanket is strong enough to hold the weight of the heaviest child in the group.

The children take places around the edge of the blanket. With the blanket on the ground, invite one child to lie down on it and be lifted gently off the ground. Do a count—"One, two, three, LIFT" and raise the blanket off the ground. Knee high is usually high enough. When lifted, the child becomes wrapped in a cozy cocoon. Rock them back and forth and then finish with "One, two, three, DOWN." Gently!

Safety Note +

Only play this if you have two or more adults who are comfortable lifting the weight of each child. Though all of the children will take part in the lifting, you cannot solely rely on them.

Chapter 9

Circle Games

Circle Games can be valuable transition tools. Since you often begin a session in a circle, with everyone on their own home spot, you can move right into one of these activities. Likewise, it is nice to end a session in a circle

if you want to wrap up with a discussion. Once your circle game is over, the children can move right into their home spots without too much effort. Transition tools or not, Circle Games are also just great fun!

Name Game

Learning names is as challenging for children as it is for adults. Children need frequent opportunities to learn their peers' names, especially if they are in a large class or if they only see each other a couple of times a week. If you have ever played the *Name Game* with adults, this is not the same. Read on...

Space   Small

Props   Two or three soft balls

How to Play

Begin the activity by tossing a ball to a child. (Be sure to have eye contact with the child before tossing it.)

When a child catches the ball, they hold it in the air and shout their name, then toss the ball to someone else in the circle. Remind the children to toss the ball *gently*. If they drop it, they should simply pick the ball up and then hold it up.

Do this until everyone has gotten the ball a couple of times.

Now play a group name challenge—as children catch the ball, they raise the ball over their head and all the other children shout their name.

Variation

After children become familiar with each others names, you can move on to the more classic version of *Name Game*. Get several balls going around at once. Now a child must call another child's name and get eye contact before tossing the ball. The receiving child then says "Thank you, _____ (the tosser's name)." Add balls to the tossing when the group is ready for a greater challenge.

The Coming and Going of the Rain

This is a useful transition game that you can use whenever you need to shift energy into a lower gear. Once the group becomes familiar with the progression of sounds you can designate a child to take on the lead role.

Space   Small

Props   None needed

How to Play

> Sit in a circle, legs outstretched and tell the group you are going to tell a story by passing a sound around the circle. Once the person on you right sees you creating the sound, they begin making the same sound. Then the person to their right begins making the sound and so on all the way around the circle. When the sound gets back to you, move on to the next sound. Be sure that the children understand that they should not make a new sound until the child next to then begins it.

> "We are going to work together to make a rain storm. We will begin with the sun shining, then the wind will begin to blow, rain drops start to fall, becoming a hard rain, then there's thunder and lightning! But that will stop and we'll only hear rain, then just wind, and finally the sun will shine again."

The progression of sounds is:

1. A happy sigh, "ahh," as we look up to the sun-shine

2. Rub both hands together, back and forth—the wind

3. Snap fingers (or light clapping for groups that can't snap their fingers)—rain drops

4. Loudly slap knees—hard rain

5. Stomp feet on the floor—thunder

Reverse the pattern:

4. Loudly slap knees

3. Snap fingers or lightly clap

2. Rub hands together

1. "Ahh," looking up to the sun

Variation

Children like to add to their own characters and sounds to the story or create their own stories. One preschool group added a coyote into the story. Who can resist an opportunity to howl at the moon?

Red Handed

I can't play this game without singing or humming, "The Wonder ball goes round and round..." But *Red Handed* is lots more fun than that old playground game, which eliminated players along the way and ended up with only one winner. Everyone is always in and everyone wins in *Red Handed*.

Props   Several small and very soft objects— fleece balls, foam balls, socks, etc. I thought stuffed animals would work well with pre-schoolers but the game ends quickly because they would rather snuggle them than pass them on!

How to Play

Have everyone sit in a circle, very close together.

Show the group the hot potatoes (balls).

The challenge is to get rid of the hot potatoes very quickly. Players can pass the potatoes in either direction but only to the children directly next to them. Balls cannot be thrown across the circle.

The object is to NOT get stuck with more than one object in your hands or lap at one time. When this happens there are screams of delight at being caught *Red Handed*, which anyone who notices will yell out loudly.

The game doesn't stop when this happens. Often some children don't even notice because they are so intent on what's happening on their side of the circle. Just keep the action going.

Start the balls moving in opposite directions using two or three at first and gradually adding one at a time as the group becomes familiar with the game.

Variation

Children like to play this game often. Four- and five-year-olds seem to do better playing *Red Handed* in one direction initially. After several rounds, try passing the balls in both directions.

Safety Note +

In the excitement of the game some children may send the objects flying across the circle or into the face of the child next to them. Call a break and reinforce their memory of the rules and ideas of being Kind and Safe.

Blanket Ball

Constant motion, unpredictable results and flying objects attract young children to this game. In my experience with preschoolers and kindergartners, this one is always on their top 10 most requested list.

Space   Large, open

Props   A large blanket, sheet, or parachute and lots of fleece balls

How to Play

Children stand in a circle or square around the blanket. Everyone reaches down and grabs the blanket with both hands, rolling some of it up to get a good, tight grip.

Raise the blanket off the ground and create waves by flapping it up and down.

Add a couple of fleece balls to the top and watch them become airborne. Add more balls one by one. When a ball goes flying off the blanket, you or one of the children can retrieve it and throw it back on. Older children sometimes like to designate one or two people to be designated retrievers.

It's fun to sit *under* the flapping blanket but you won't have to tell your children that. They'll figure it out themselves pretty quickly.

Safety Note +

Use only objects that are as soft as or softer than fleece balls.

Cat and Mouse Tag

This game often takes several attempts before all the children really understand their roles. Everyone loves being in the middle, so make sure you have enough time to give everyone at least one opportunity to be a cat or a mouse.

Space   Small

Props   Blindfolds (optional)

How to Play

Create a circle of children kneeling on the ground or on a circle of cushions and pillows if you only have a few children.

Two children come into the middle of the circle. One becomes the mouse the other becomes the cat. Have them practice their respective squeaks and meows. Both children will be blindfolded or just close their eyes—whichever they prefer.

When you say "Go," the cat will try to find the mouse and the mouse will quietly try to avoid an encounter with the cat. All players need to be quiet on the outer circle.

The outer children are there to guide the cat or mouse back into the circle if they start heading out. Occasionally you can ask the cat and mouse to give their squeak and meow to help them gauge where their foe is located.

When the cat finds the mouse, have the children switch roles or pick two new players. Between rounds discuss ways that cats can find their mouse and ways the mouse can be extra quiet.

Sidebar Note

Whether children are blindfolded or close their eyes, they will find a way to peek if they feel the need. Let the peeking happen. Remember: they are challenging themselves by choice.

Children on the perimeter of the circle will often have a hard time keeping quiet. You may need to be on the move on the outside of the circle to act as coach for players inside and out. It's worth sticking with the game even if it seems that it is not going as it should. Little by little they pick up on the various roles.

Speed Rabbit

Preschoolers and kindergartners love to create animals for this game and simply run through the animal signs as you call out the animal. Older children can work in teams to create the animal signs as quickly as they can.

Space   Small

Props   None

How to Play

Stand or sit in a circle. Together create animal signs for three or four animals. For example, the sign for CAT might be fingers making whiskers off the cheeks. RABBIT might be long ears made by outstretched arms over the head. FROG could be a squatting position with hands flat on the ground.

Have everyone slap their knees, as in a drums roll, to increase the activity level and create a sense of speed. Then call out an animal name.

Children must quickly make the appropriate animal sign. Go right back into the fast knee slapping and then call out another animal name. Continue to increase the speed of the your animal names until you bring the game to completion with rapid fire animal names.

Variations

Pairs Speed Rabbit

A more challenging variation is *Pairs Speed Rabbit*. Begin the game by pairing up. As above, work with the group to create animal signs that they will perform in teams.

This is a group team-building activity in itself. Not only do they exercise their creativity, but they also must come to agreement as a group as to what will be the sign for each animal.

Once you have agreement on three or four animals you can begin the speed aspect of the game. Stand in the middle of the circle of pairs. Spin around with your arm pointing out to the circle. When you stop spinning, call out an animal name. The pair you are pointing to must create the animal sign before you finish counting to 10.

You can vary the speed of your counting according to the pairs ability to create their animal sign. If the pair does not complete their animal before you get to 10, one of them can come into the middle to be the pointer. You may need to stay in the middle to help the pointer. Very often they will forget to count to 10. When the group has become proficient at the initial animal signs add a few more.

Speed Rabbit/Twizzle Combo

If your group has played both *Speed Rabbit* and *Twizzle* separately, try adding animal signs into your commands for *Twizzle*. It's especially fun to call out the animal name then immediately yell "FREEZE!"

Beach Ball Tunnel

This old classic used to be done as a relay race in a straight line which, of course, you can still do. But it works well as a group circle challenge.

Space   Small

Props   Several beach balls, sponge balls or playground balls

How to Play

Create a circle of children, one behind the other and all facing in the same direction. The first child sends a ball under their legs to the next player who passes it under their legs, and so on around the circle.

Once the group is comfortable with the task you can introduce one or two more balls so the level of activity is continuous.

Variations

One child can kick the ball as far as possible. The group then runs to their ball and forms a circle. Have the group select the person who will be the ball picker-upper, otherwise, competition to retrieve the ball will break down the spirit of fun and cooperation. Forming the circle will be quite a challenge for some groups.

Group Bocci

I especially enjoyed playing this game after agroup made their own bean bags. The children gets a great sense of satisfaction in making their own props. Add more of your own bean bags so that children develop their *Bocci* skills before worrying about retrieving their own beanbags from the circle.

Space   Medium, open

Props   Bean bags, fleece balls or trash balls, 2 or 3 per child. One hula hoop, tape or rope.

How to Play

Create concentric circles starting with a hoop in the center. Add one or two larger circles around the hoop using ropes or tape.

The children stand in a circle around the concentric circles at a distance that seems comfortable for them.

Give everyone a bean bag and tell them that the goal is for the group to get as many bean bags into the circles as possible.

The center hoop is obviously the most difficult to land in. As the children develop their tossing skills they will increase the number of bean bags in the center.

Play several rounds moving the children further away from the circles as their throwing skills improve.

Variations

Assign points to each circle, the highest number of points to the center circle. Once children have tossed their balls or bean bags, conduct a math lesson to calculate a total group score. Play another round and have the group set a goal for the number of points they believe they can score.

Vertical Bocci

This is a combination of *Group Bocci* and *Help Me, Please* with a vertical twist! After playing both of these games, go for *Vertical Bocci*.

Space   Medium, open

Props   Lots of balls, one hoop or several hoops taped together (I tape them side by side so they look like the Olympic rings, but usually fewer.)

How to Play

Give each child 2 or 3 balls. Have them stand behind a line or rope. Hold the hoop or network of hoops vertically, or suspend them between two posts or trees. The challenge is to toss all the balls through the hoops from behind a line (or standing on designated home spots).

I like to let the children randomly aim at a target for a while. During this time, everyone throws at the same time and retrieves at the same time.

When the group is ready to play, choose two children to be retrievers. Let 2 or 3 children toss their balls at a time attempting to get them through a hoop. The retrievers deposit the ones that go through hoops into a bucket. They return the balls that missed to the throwers (any thrower will do). Play continues until all the balls have passed through the hoops.

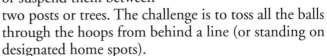

Project Adventure
Services and Publications

Services

Project Adventure, Inc. is a national, non-profit corpora-
tion dedicated to helping schools, youth groups, camps,
corporations, counseling groups, physical education
programs and others implement Project Adventure ideas.
Characterized by an atmosphere that is fun, supportive
and challenging, Project Adventure programs use non-
competitive games, group problem-solving Initiatives
and ropes course events as the principal activities to help
individuals reach their goals; to improve self-esteem, to
develop strategies that enhance decision making, and to
learn to respect differences within a group. Toward these
ends, the following services are available:

Project Adventure Workshops

Through a network of national certified trainers, Project
Adventure conducts workshops for teachers, counselors,
youth workers, and other professionals who work with
people. These workshops are given in various sections of
the country. Separate workshops are offered in Project
Adventure Games and Initiatives, Challenge Ropes
Course Skills, Counseling Theory and Techniques for
Adventure Based Programs, and Interdisciplinary Aca-
demic Curriculum.

Challenge Course Design and Installation

Project Adventure has been designing and installing
ropes courses (a series of individual and group challenge
elements situated indoors in a gymnasium or outdoors
in trees) since 1971. PA Staff can travel to your site and

design/install a course appropriate for your needs and budget.

Equipment Sales

A catalog service of hard-to-find props, materials and tools used in adventure programs and the installation and use of Challenge Ropes Courses.

Corporate Programs

Management workshops for business people and professionals. These workshops are designed for increasing efficiency of team members in the workplace. The trust, communication, and risk-taking ability learned in these programs translate into a more cohesive and productive team at work.

Program Accreditation

The Accreditation process is an outside review of a program by PA staff. Programs that undertake the accreditation process are seeking outside evaluation with regard to quality and safety. The term accreditation means "formal written confirmation." Programs seeking confirmation are looking to ensure that they are within the current standards of safety and risk management. This assurance may be useful for making changes in program equipment and/or design, and in providing information on program quality to third parties such as administrators, insurance companies and the public.

To Contact Project Adventure

> Project Adventure has several overseas offices, including Australia, New Zealand, Japan, Singapore and Taiwan. For further information, contact PA headquarters:

U.S. Offices

Project Adventure, Inc.

> P.O. Box 100
> Hamilton, MA 01936
>
> TEL: 978/468-7981
> FAX: 978/468-7605

Southeast

> P.O. Box 2447
> Covington, GA 30015
>
> TEL: 770/784-9310
> FAX:770/787-7764

West Coast

> P.O. Box 14171
> Portland, OR 97293
>
> TEL: 503/239-0169
> FAX: 503/236-6765

Vermont

> P.O.Box 1640
> Brattleboro, VT 05302
>
> TEL: 802/254-5054
> FAX: 802/254-5182

Publications

If you would like to obtain additional copies of this book, an order form is provided on the next page. Project Adventure also publishes many books in related areas. Described below are some of our best sellers, which can be ordered on the same form. Call or write to Project Adventure for a complete publications list.

QuickSilver

Adventure Games, Initiative Problems, Trust Activities and a Guide to Effective Leadership

This latest offering from cooperative games master Karl Rohnke contains over 150 new games, problem solving initiatives, ice breakers, variations on old standards, trust, closures and more. There is also a section on leadership with co-author, Steve Butler, in which they impart many of the secrets that they use when leading and designing programs.

by Karl Rohnke and Steve Butler

Cowstails and Cobras II

Karl Rohnke's classic guide to games, Initiative problems and Adventure activities. Offering a thorough treatment of Project Adventure's philosophy and approach to group activities, *Cowstails II* provides both the experienced practitioner and the novice with a unique and valuable resource.

By Karl Rohnke

Silver Bullets

More Initiative problems, Adventure games and trust activities from Karl Rohnke: 165 great games and activities that require few, if any, props. Use this as a companion to *Cowstails and Cobras II* or a stand alone guide to invigorate your program.

By Karl Rohnke

Youth Leadership In Action

All too often young people have little access to the resources necessary to improve their skills and develop their leadership potential. *Youth Leadership In Action* addresses this need by providing a guide for youth leaders to implement experiential, cooperative activities and techniques into their programs.

But the most striking and unique feature of this book is that it was written by a group of youth leaders. This group of eight leaders have taken 54 of Project Adventure's most popular Adventure games and activities and rewritten the instructions and rules in the way they present and play them. They also give a brief history of Project Adventure, present their own definition of Adventure, and explain some of PA's basic concepts and techniques — Full Value Contract, Challenge By Choice, debriefing, sequencing, etc. They also provide a section on effective leadership and how to start several types of programs.

Edited by Steve Fortier

Order Form

Ship to:

Name _____

Address (no P.O. Box nos.) _____

_____

City _____ State ____ Zip _____

Phone(_____) _____ Ext _____

Due to the inability to trace Parcel Post shipments, it is our policy to ship U.S. orders via UPS.
We must have a UPS shipping address (no Post Office box numbers).

Book Rate will be used for orders sent to foreign countries and in cases of insufficient street addresses.

Payment: ❏ Check   ❏ MasterCard   ❏ VISA

Credit Card # _____ Exp. ___ / ___

Signature _____
(Signature required for all charge orders.)

TO ORDER PLEASE CALL: 800/795-9039   FAX: 978/524-4600
or return this form to: **Project Adventure, Inc.**
P.O. Box 100
Hamilton, MA 01936

Qty.	Title	ISBN	Cost	Total
	Youth Leadership in Action	0107-3	15.00	
	QuickSilver	0032-8	25.00	
	Silver Bullets	5682-X	22.00	
	Adventure Play	1420-5	16.00	
	Cowstails II	5434-7	22.00	

* **TAX-EXEMPT** orders must be accompanied by a copy of the purchaser's certificate of tax exemption.

How to Calculate Shipping Charges

■ **Add $4.00** for first book.
■ **Add .50c** for each additional book up to 5 books.
■ **Over 5 books,** add 5% of total.

On books being shipped to AK, HI, Canada
and foreign countries:
• 4.50 to Alaska & Hawaii
• 6.50 to Canada
• 7.00 on foreign orders
On orders of 5 or more books, call Project
Adventure for exact shipping cost.

Subtotal _____

Please add sales tax:
GA add 6%
VT & MA add 5%   _____

Tax Exempt No.*   _____

Shipping (instructions at left)   _____

TOTAL   _____